THE
TECHNIQUES
OF
CREATIVE
THINKING

How to use your ideas
to achieve success

by Robert P. Crawford

author of THINK FOR YOURSELF and
DIRECT CREATIVITY

USE OF QUOTATIONS

Because of the help and encouragement Crawford's works have offered thousands of people the world over, and our desire so to continue, we maintain a more liberal policy on quotations than do most publishers.

Quotations 75 words or less are permitted without charge provided credit is given to the authors.

Quotations 75 to 150 words are permitted without charge provided credit is given to the author and the book from which derived.

Quotations 150 to 250 words are permitted without charge provided credit is given to the author, the book concerned, and the present publisher, Fraser Publishing Company, Box 494, Burlington, Vermont 05402.

Send copies of quotations to the publisher.

For quotations of more than 250 words, digests, and foreign translations, a royalty is charged. Write the publishers.

FRASER PUBLISHING COMPANY, BURLINGTON, VERMONT

Printed in the U.S.A.

Contents

CONTENTS

THE TECHNIQUES OF CREATIVE THINKING

How to Use Your Ideas to Achieve Success

{1

The Age of Ideas

THIS IS THE AGE OF IDEAS. Everywhere you turn, you are reminded of it.

Down the avenue you walk—no, you don't walk; you ride in your streamlined new car—and what do you see?

The new office buildings almost of solid glass.

The new church with its severely modernistic walls.

The shop windows full of television sets and the roofs of the houses covered with television aerials.

The women with this year's "new look."

And, farther out, the thousands of new-style houses—so new they would have shocked the mansion builders of the twenties.

You pick up a magazine, and what do you see? Not only are the stories and articles new ideas in themselves but so are the advertisements. They sell everything from automatic washing machines to decay-fighting tooth paste. More than that, innumerable advertisements come right out and refer to the idea business itself with such thoughts as "Helping Hand for an Idea Man," "A Small Company with a Big Idea" and "Scrambling for an Idea."

Everywhere—

Newness, newness, newness.

Brightness, brightness, brightness.

Smartness, smartness, smartness.

Usefulness, usefulness, usefulness.

Little ideas and big ideas. Everybody with an idea or hoping to get one. Revolutionary ideas such as radar and atomic power. Ideas that help us lead the lazy life. Ideas that make our lives more pleasant and resultful. Ideas to make things safer. Ideas that cost us money and ideas that make us money. Even "dumb ideas" that succeed just because they are dumb.

This is the Idea Age. *An Idea Age for the many* and not just for the few whose names are destined to be in the history books.

And you, sitting there in your easy chair, want to get in on this idea business. You are tired of everyone else creating ideas for you to buy or follow. You want to create some ideas for yourself or, better still, for the other fellow.

Perhaps I should put it in another way. You already have some ideas. Most people do. But maybe they are "not so hot." You want to have better ideas and you want what ideas you do have to succeed better.

Some people think of the idea business as a game. And it is. Others think of it as a life and death struggle. And it is that, too, for countless men and businesses.

What brought us the Idea Age?

It was not always this way. Not such a great number of years ago, Alex Osborn, the famous advertising man, and I were walking uptown from his New York offices. I had been holding classes since 1931 in creative thinking—or "the idea business"—at the University of Nebraska, and Osborn had been holding similar classes for a long time in his own organization where he had some five hundred employees responsible for creative work.

He was bemoaning the fact that over the years people generally had been so unreceptive to the tremendous possibilities of creative thought. "When you started out, I thought you were away ahead of your time," he remarked to me, "and I still think you are." I think he was ahead of his time also. We were two men with an idea that people ought to have more ideas.

Now it has changed. The idea business has become big business.

Why the idea boom? The answer is that civilization has finally come to the conclusion that it must have ideas. "I want new ideas. I don't know what the future has in store for me, but if I am called to a high position of responsibility, I will want new ideas." Thus does David Lawrence report what General Eisenhower told him in a pre-election interview.

And not only civilization as a whole but each of us as an individual needs ideas. The Dow-Jones service describes the man without an idea as a GLILG, a getting-lost-in-the-lurch guy.

But a more significant reason for the idea boom is the fact that thousands of people have learned that "they can do it too." In the past, men surrounded the process with a halo of mystery and with explanations that "just a few people have it." Such statements have been simply an admission that most individuals did not understand how the process worked or how one might be able to direct the process oneself. Psychologists were partly responsible for this situation since they were slow to recognize that creative thinking and, especially, plain ordinary idea production are possible for the average person. While they were working with other branches of psychology, creative thinking was kept largely on the shelf. They were not sure that they could lay down the rules of the game.

Dr. J. P. Guilford, in his presidential address to the American Psychological Association in 1950, pointed out that of 121,000 titles listed in the index of *Psychological Abstracts* in 23 years, only 186 were classified as definitely bearing on the subject of creativity. "The neglect of this subject by psychologists is appalling," he declared.

Many world leaders sensed the peculiar situation. Something like a gold mine was at hand, and no one was digging out the gold. C. Spearman of the University of London had been looking into it. Henry Suzzallo, president of the Carnegie Foundation for the Advancement of Teaching, told me years ago that here was an educational "job to be done." DeWitt Wallace, publisher of the *Reader's Digest*, put some time and money into these efforts.

In the final analysis it was probably the businessmen of the country who did most of the work on the subject. They simply went ahead and by trial and error began to produce results. Suggestion systems found a place in corporate life. These systems were receiving places for ideas from nonprofessionals even if the process of creating ideas was not generally available. Businessmen found that they could succeed equally well in widely diverse lines of activity once they had the fundamental idea.

Then people who were not inventors began to invent things. Chemists who were not doctors turned out famous new medicines. Lest this all seem to be a topsy-turvy procedure, we must ask the reader's indulgence until he has gone many more pages in the book and learned how such things are possible.

World War II was more than a succession of battles and engagements; it was also a battle of ideas—not only the ideas of important military and political figures, but the ideas of tens of thousands of ordinary people who perhaps had never before seen one of their ideas in actual use. With the advent of World War II, the search for ideas became a vigorous one. "Ideas invent new things." "Ideas save time and materials." "Ideas win wars." The period of World War II became an era when creative thought was at a premium.

Even a National Inventors' Council was established in Washington, D.C. During the war it received information on more than 200,000 inventions and interviewed nearly 14,-000 inventors. Five thousand inventions were considered of enough value to be carefully reviewed by the various branches of the armed services.

During two and a half years of wartime operations the War Department estimated savings to the government from its suggestion system reached the astonishing total of $153,859,236. The Ordnance Department, working with its own employees, estimated it saved $50,000,000 in one year alone from suggestions within the organization. One-half of all the ideas offered were adopted.

Occasionally a very great idea came to light. It is estimated that R. L. Graumann's Navy suggestion regarding time fuses saved the government in just one year the enormous sum of $23,000,000.

It was a different story from that of World War I. Then, the Naval Consulting Board and the Inventors' Section of the General Staff asked for ideas. The Navy felt, after it was all over, that possibly it had not been worth while for, out of 110,000 proposals, only around one-tenth of 1 per cent were considered worthy of further investigation.

But in World War II idea production was better systematized through the growing personnel sections of the various government branches, and instead of receiving only the "revolutionary but impractical" ideas which so many beginners conjure up, the government was able to put to use thousands of little ideas. Each idea may have saved only a few hundred dollars a year, but the total was enormous.

Donald Nelson, then chairman of the War Production Board, described this period thus: "Magnificent things have been brought to light. Men have made contributions that are now closely guarded military secrets. They are of that importance. But these great improvements do not measure the power of this weapon. The millions of little improvements that save an hour or a pound of brass make it devastating. In their aggregate these will amass our production victory."

And so it was!

During a great war, ideas are essential to victory and to production. After a war, they become even more necessary because companies and individuals survive only as they find ideas to fit themselves to a changing civilization. Companies and men that cannot create things are left out. Those that create things may go so far as to leave their names in the history of their times. A man with a supply of ideas fears nothing for he has become the master of his own future.

Today is open hunting season for ideas. Over 5,000 American companies maintain suggestion systems for the consideration of ideas submitted by employees. There is even a National Association of Suggestion Systems with headquarters in Chicago. General Motors is securing about 30,-000 *usable* ideas from its employees each year. And, mind you, just about one out of every four ideas submitted is usable. To date, it has paid out over $9,000,000 for suggestions from employees. No one can say that ordinary men and women cannot think up new things.

In the Navy, in one recent year, the department *adopted* some 21,000 suggestions, or better than one out of every four submitted. The Navy's idea business is now four times as brisk as it was in 1944, a war year.

Periods when the world is shaken up, when people are going here, there, and everywhere, are always periods for new ideas. Boom eras are boom times for ideas. Thousands of them are kept in storage by individuals and industry for later use.

There is an interesting financial consideration in the production of ideas that many companies and men do not appreciate. It results from high-income taxes. It may seem strange to credit taxes with such miracles as idea creation, but here is the way it multiplies the idea business tremendously. Any corporation or individual charges off all business expenses against taxable income. Naturally, this includes the heavy expense of getting new things going. During its early years, a new idea in production may actually lose money. But the company or individual pays for all this initial expense with twenty-five- to fifty-cent dollars, for, if it did not spend the money on such "new things," it would be paying a good part of it in income tax.

The theory behind such a procedure is that one is buying a successful future at low cost. In the years to come income tax should decline and, at the same time, the new idea should be in full swing and making a profit. Finally, really big money may roll in as a result of it.

When you examine the financial pages of a magazine you may be surprised to note that many companies offered for sale present as an advantage the fact that they are losing money. Another corporation buys a company to cut down its own taxes now and hopes eventually to have enough bright ideas to make long-term gains.

Individuals follow the same policy in carrying out important projects in the field of investment, the making of inventions, and similar things. Thousands of men and women have in readiness for the future a great stock of new things waiting for the propitious moment.

There is another factor that is producing an idea race in America. No new scientific idea or process stays new very long. Indeed, if it is a good one, it may be so successful and there may be so many imitators that a point of diminishing returns may be reached. Then the only thing that can save companies is still more ideas. By their very success they are forced to better and better ideas.

I can remember only a comparatively few years ago when

a group of men living in a military billet in Tokyo had to take up a collection to buy penicillin to save the life of a servant. And it meant five or ten dollars from every man. Yet, as I write, only a few years later, penicillin has become a real "drug on the market." *The Wall Street Journal* recently reported that in nine years the price had declined to one-four-thousandth of the original price.

Or turn to the frozen food industry. You remember those enticing advertisements of not so many years ago and how proudly you carried home that little carton of "fresh strawberries." Today the great problem is not just too many frozen strawberries but too much of nearly every type of frozen product. "No one is making any money in the business," says one dealer.

It is this rapid growth in civilization that uproots civilization every few years. Not long ago a broker's newsletter called attention to the great number of one-time famous names that no longer are favored in the stock market. Their products are sound and good. But the financial statistician concluded that it is so easy for competitive products to arise and shine that the old-timers without some new idea or approach can no longer exert dominance in the field.

This ability of the individual to cope with change must increase these days. "On December 17, 1903, began an era which we have called the Air Age," remarked General James H. Doolittle. "It has changed our thinking, our habits, our transport, our mails, our commerce, our industry, our agriculture—and our wars. But more significant, the first fifty years of powered flight have brought the world abruptly into what can be termed the Age of Wonders. This new era is with us now. In the field of air transportation, we are on the verge of keeping pace with the sun."

What Ideas Can Do for You

But here you are, just ordinary Smith or Jones, and you are in the individual greased idea race instead of the corporation greased idea race. And that pig of an idea is mighty hard to get a hold on.

Ask yourself: "What do I want out of ideas?"

Money? Yes, many people have accumulated fortunes through ideas.

Keep your small business going up instead of down? Yes, many an idea has made a business.

Fun of seeing things succeed? Yes, one has to have some success to avoid frustration and keep one's mental health.

Make your country a better place in which to live? Yes, schools, churches, hospitals, towns, and cities need ideas.

Keep the world in better trim? Thousands of downtrodden people need ideas more than anything else.

For ideas are the world's motive power.

Most people, it is true, are going to be interested in the financial aspects of the matter. In plain English, they want dollars and cents. That is not an unworthy ambition, for anyone who has known people knows that the lack of money is quite as often the root of evil as the love of money. Yes, people want ideas to use in their occupations. They may seek to create some invention or new line of work that will make their future more promising. Or it may be that they are interested in doing better at their present jobs.

Ideas often get the job in the first place. "You can be

either a man or woman for this job as long as you are bristling with ideas," reads one help-wanted advertisement, "and sufficiently organized to see them through."

"The type of person my client is seeking will not be too easy to find," reads another advertisement. "He must be a developer and maker of things. This man might be a model-maker or supervise the making of models and developing of devices. He might be a man trained in practical design. He might be a designer of displays or gadgets. He might be a man who is good at freehand drawing and makes things with his hands as a hobby, or a man who has had original training as an artisan (someone who understands the possibilities of metals), perhaps a college graduate who became a production engineer. But whatever he does he *must* be someone who has the ability to work with his hands and who enjoys this phase of creating things which he himself can carry forward to completion. My client is completely open-minded regarding compensation but he has a reputation for being generous so that the right man might earn anywhere up to $10- $15- $20,000. This is an unusual request for an unusual man." In other words, the company is seeking a creator.

How many times do you find the requirement for a really high-priced position that of furnishing ideas! It is clearly evident that if your ideas are going to make a company $15,000 a year in net profit, the company is not going to worry so much about paying you $7,500. Invariably, when you are applying for a really important job, you will be asked, "What can you do for the business?" And that means simply the supplying of ideas. The most appreciated idea that anyone can contribute to any business is one that will increase sales or decrease costs of production. It is the quickest road to promotion and success.

So keenly do great corporations feel about this matter of creativity that they are making particular efforts to find those individuals in their ranks who are capable of making very special contributions along this line. General Electric at Schenectady maintains a course in this subject for promising employees. The AC Spark Plug division of General Motors is thinking along this line with some psychological studies under way. In the great new field of creative engineering, the Massachusetts Institute of Technology is in the lead with several courses. The University of Southern California has been carrying out government research looking toward psychological tests for people with creative ability. I receive many letters from high executives of corporations who want to do more with this enticing and profitable subject.

But, as you read this book, you will find that I go a considerable distance beyond the thinking of many corporations. I maintain that this creative power is lying unused in nearly all individuals and may be increased, once the individual knows how. "Like most behavior, creative activity probably represents to some extent many learned skills," says Professor Guilford at the University of Southern California. "There may be limitations set on these skills by heredity, but I am convinced that through learning one can extend the skills within those limitations. The least that we can do is to remove the blocks that are often in the way. Everyone can be creative to some degree in many ways. Recognizing this simple truth is an important beginning. Knowing what the aspects of creative thinking are is another big step. The rest depends upon practice, practice, practice. Society's responsibility is to provide favorable environment and education and the appropriate rewards for creative production."

Some people do not need ideas for financial success. Perhaps, fortunately, they have already attained that success. Perhaps, like the businessman who has retired or the secretary who married the boss, they want something pleasant to do.

My point is that the idea business is also a valuable avocation for the retired businessman or woman or for the person in a hospital. It enables you to turn time—anywhere, any place—into a valuable and productive article. This matter of discovering ideas is the most satisfying way of occupying your time, since you never know when you may be striking fascinating pay dirt. It is mental prospecting.

A young man who writes successfully from time to time for the *Saturday Evening Post* wrote me the other day about his need for ideas. When a writer feels bogged down, when he has "gone stale," the thing to do is to play with creating ideas. Soon he will find that he has created new ideas worth far more than those with which he had been working. It will do your mind good to play in previously unexplored fields. Such a course leads to priceless adventures in the mind's capacity to invent. Nothing will give a man such a mental lift—"take him out of the dumps"—as the feeling that he has created something.

People underprivileged either by race or individual status often have to make use of unusual ideas to overcome their handicaps. Of course all people are "underprivileged" in one way or another when compared with someone else, and consequently everyone has to improve his or her position. The best way of doing so is by means of ideas.

Ideas enable you to find your place in life, for, without ideas, you will usually have to remain where circumstances have put you.

You Influence the World

If there are opportunities to benefit the individual there are also opportunities to benefit the world. In a way this is a demonstration of how the world moves. It moves through ideas—good, bad, and indifferent ones, as far as the impact on others is concerned.

New ideas do possess within themselves the power to re-make a world. Great Britain has, for example, set up a National Research Development Corporation "out of the observation that, while the ingenuity of British inventors was second to none, adoption of the results of their discovery and invention was frequently slower in this country (England) than abroad." Its object is to benefit the British economy by "facilitating the introduction of nationally valuable inventions into use as soon as possible and also by exploiting them overseas to the national advantage."

Ideas have the power to eliminate the causes of discord and strife within nations and between peoples. Most troubles arise because countries and peoples want more than they have of material goods. One way is to reach out and take them away from others by force. Another way is to develop such good ideas that wants are abundantly satisfied. The United States does not have to reach out and seize others' possessions; rather, it is capable of inventing and producing a large proportion of the things it needs.

How few backward countries appreciate the significance of this fact! The "have-nots" are more often lacking in ideas than in material resources. In the Orient a while back I found a machine company decently enough equipped. The Japanese had gone away leaving millions of yen in its treasury. But the "new management," with no ideas of what to do, had merely used up the millions with nothing to show for it. Never was there greater need in the world than now for ideas. The United States may be discouraging the ingenuity of the world by dumping the results of ideas upon it rather than by directing the ability of countries to create their own ideas and solve their own problems.

In this idea business you are a partner with the world as well as with your associates. Your own creation of ideas may be made the happiest of undertakings and productive of personal, monetary, and spiritual satisfaction.

Creative thinking is today's most prized, profit-producing possession for any individual, corporation, or country. It has the capacity to change you, your business, and the world. But the process, as we are going to find out, is not so formidable or difficult as has often been thought. We now propose in succeeding chapters to show how you may learn to create worth-while ideas quickly, readily, and in great number. Perhaps you will change yourself, your business, or maybe the world itself.

{2

Your Magic Future

My ASIATIC FRIEND said to me: "We must run swiftly; we must go as far in five years as you in America have gone in 50 years."

The man over there on the other side of the world might as well have said: "We must try to create and carry out as many bright ideas in five years as you Americans have in 50."

My friend gave good advice to all of us. These days everyone, no matter in what part of the world he lives, has to run swiftly. Or, as Carl E. Holmes puts it: "Our business in life is not to get ahead of others but to get ahead of ourselves—to break our own records—to improve our own methods and to do our work better than we have ever done it before."

Everywhere, people and industries and governments, usually unconscious of the process, are trying to break over into a new future. "We need ideas, not money," Mohammed Ali, a well-known lawyer of Pakistan, told Americans when he visited this country. Ideas put into action become events, and they count in our own lives and the life of the world.

But we are concerned with our own ideas and events. And that means, of course, our own personal future. Let us try to find our own future. It is a magic future that starts and grows in our own minds. It may pick up any one of us and carry his name into posterity.

Some years ago I thought of this business of creating ideas as something very mysterious. Like many others, I believed that it could not be developed, that it either happened or did not happen. But I soon found that creation was a process. I found that certain university students could develop this power and that, as they did so, they became resourceful.

It is as foolish to say that the process of creative thought cannot be taught as to say that medicine or engineering cannot be taught. There is a reason for anything that happens in the world. We can find the reason. When we actually learn how, it is an easy matter to go ahead and make things happen.

Creation, around which we have always placed an aura of mystery, consists in turning the mind forward. Few of us have ever learned the art of thinking forward, because education and experience have always emphasized thinking backward. Strange to say, in most of our educational processes, we deal rather consistently with the past, but without much definite understanding as to how it fits the future. We remember, remember, and then remember some more. But the real object of this remembering is to give ourselves a better future, unless we are to do like so many thousands about us and crawl back into the past for safety's sake.

The great names in the world, however, are those of men and women who have moved forward. Without the comparatively few hundred men like Watt, Pasteur, and Einstein, civilization as we know it would not exist. Ideas have made the world.

The strange thing is that I, we, you—most of us—have done so little. In nearly every office there are individuals—men and women—on very modest salaries, always reported to have "bright minds." In those same offices are other men on relatively high salaries who seem to be taking life easy. In most cases the high-priced men and women are those who have the knack of furnishing their companies with bright, new ideas. These are not always so-called "brilliant" men and women. I venture to say that many of the poorly paid would top more successful men and women in intelligence tests. I see all about me people who were known as very brilliant individuals in school, who were graduated from universities with honors, and yet to whom nothing seems to have happened. Look about for yourself.

Again I say that the difficulty in getting into this practice of creation is that our existence up to now has often been opposed to it. It is almost as if there were a constant battle between past and future. We see and feel our past but not our future. Education usually studies the past, but emphasis upon the past, unless we make use of it, is almost directly opposed to creative thought. We have made too much of a mystery of the future. Yet ideas put into execution *are* the future.

Progress—what is it but a succession of ideas put into effect and piled one on top of the other? A progressive age is an age in which there is a multiplicity of these changes. A progressive company is one that creates and executes many ideas. Ages, companies, and individuals that originate few things are backward. Without these new ideas and consequent changes all of us would be living in a world no different from the times before Christ—even like the days of the caveman.

We Begin to Begin

This chapter is taking you scarcely ten minutes to read. It is intended to be short—to get you out into the actual business of idea production as rapidly as possible. It is important that we produce as many ideas as possible. To make a satisfactory contribution to the world or a contribution to ourselves we must produce ideas.

Undoubtedly some of my readers may have already sensed profound implications in what we are considering. More and more of these implications will come upon you as you proceed. But, as far as this book is concerned, we shall leave consideration of these philosophical matters—the influence of what we are doing upon the world itself—until the later chapters. In the meantime, we shall be starting our idea factory.

Now *your* job begins. One of the purposes of this book is to proceed rapidly, to tell only the necessary facts, and then to ask you to turn these over in your mind, adding to the subject further facts and conclusions from your own experience. This book depends for its success on how you work with it. This is primarily *your* book; you create things as you proceed.

First of all, I want you to get a little pocket notebook. This is to be your notebook, not mine. You are to carry it with you. It is not to be the customary notebook of the school or college student who puts down everything he is told, keeps it sacred, and then returns it to the instructor wholly unread at the end of the semester. Rather, this little notebook is to contain your ideas and observations, the great number of things you will learn to pick up as you go through the book. These ideas will come to you here, there, and everywhere, hours or days after you have studied the particular chapter before you.

What are you going to create? You may, of course, work in many different lines. There is no monopoly on ideas or on original thinking. But the probabilities are that, at the start, many of them will be in the area in which you are now engaged.

Right at this point it will do you good to think of your ultimate ambition in the world. What are you really trying to do? What do you want to accomplish? After you have thought this over for a few days, write it down in the notebook. With this ambition in the back of your mind, you may find that many of your ideas will take shape in that direction.

Of course not all ideas have to take shape in line with our life's ambition. Thousands of valuable—very valuable—ideas happen along the way, as we shall see later. But it is worth while for us to have a thought starter occasionally to jolt us out of complacency.

Look back over you life and note how many really important, worth-while things have happened to you.

We've all had some really nice bits of success in our lives, bright spots that shine out with real consequence like searchlights in our ordinary existence. How did these come about? Did the old gentleman suddenly appear from the front office and say, "Well done, thou faithful servant, here's $10,000 for you"?

No, it was not like that at all, aside from a few meritorious cases where Lady Luck seemed to have been helping more than usual. The things that really counted toward success were ideas that finally set in motion a whole chain of useful and profitable events.

How many good ideas have you had in your life? Or have you just kept on going? Are you like a young man who said to me: "Life is just a series of installment payments?" What an unpleasant way to measure life!

We are setting out upon an idea safari. We are hunting not in deepest Africa but right in the jungle of our own lives. We should be dead set upon shooting down at least a few ideas. And instead of mounting these hunting trophies in our living room we want to translate them into events— events worth looking forward to and events worth looking back upon in our later years.

What kind of ideas and events shall they be? No doubt pleasant, of course. No one desires to build a life out of things that are manifestly unpleasant. It is true, of course, that unpleasant and unhappy affairs do constitute milestones. But they are negative ones. Unpleasant events, even when forgotten by our minds, become festering mental sores, as many psychoanalysts assert. Unpleasant things may come anyway, but no one should deliberately seek such things. "Put that down," I hear you say, "let's make it a pleasant event."

What else now? "Well, it certainly ought to be something worth while," you tell me. All right then, a pleasant worthwhile idea, with real consequences in future years, and you should look to the future in choosing it.

James H. Rand used to say that the way to determine what to do first was to look at the tasks from the standpoint of ten years hence. The job that will have real consequences over the years is the first to tackle *now*. But most of us do the opposite. We are so bogged down in trivialities that they consume our creative powers. Will your idea seem as worth while, or nearly as worth while, in ten years as it does now?

Next, I do not think such an event should be too easy. There is not, however, much danger of this—strokes of luck or fortune happen very seldom. But you should enjoy the feel of the oars pulling toward the shore. The perfect event gives you an incentive toward which to work.

And finally, most important of all, it should be *something that can actually be accomplished*. In working with students in the field of creative thought, the criticism often is the impracticability of their ideas. That does not mean that many great thinkers have not set to work on almost unfathomable tasks and have not actually accomplished them, but they are exceptions. Many people conceive needs, but often they are not real needs, and the means of filling them are impracticable. Let's get something, then, on which we can work with a fair indication that success will greet us.

I know a man who has specialized in small but very successful investments, each one of which is an idea. He doesn't think in big figures; he thinks in terms of small investments of $6,000 or $8,000. I doubt if he has ever had $10,000 in any one place; yet he has accumulated a considerable fortune on which he could retire very comfortably.

If he has purchased stocks cheaply, he withdraws in the boom period the amount of his original investment and lets the balance go on working. He is astute at real estate. He chooses pieces where he is sure of an increase in value and yet where the return is handsome and permanent. He has to look closely and wait for such things, but they do turn up. Each piece is an idea—an idea that most people do not see. The property pays for itself in ten or twelve years and is worth more than he originally paid—sometimes two or three times as much. But, after only a few years' operation, he is able to pay himself back the original investment out of the excess of earnings over interest charges. Finally he has an equity, or in some cases the entire property paid for; yet his original investment is little or nothing. I term him an all-round handy man with money, and that is what he is. Money accumulation is seldom luck. There are usually ideas behind it.

It may be that you will have many good ideas and you will keep them all simmering away in your idea kettle until one of them proves a great success. Edwin Perkins recently disposed of his interest in million-dollar Kool-Aid to the General Foods Corporation. But he got his start out in Hendley, Nebraska, where with boyish enthusiasm he tried the mail order business of small bottles of perfume and the printing of calling cards. Finally he developed some 125 different household items. But the outstanding success was Kool-Aid, a refreshing drink made from a concentrate and sold in small envelopes. So successful was this side of the venture that it was necessary to move it to Chicago where the factory had to be tripled in size in 1934 and doubled in both 1939 and 1949.

Middle age particularly requires the creation of ideas. If you are over 50 years of age, you must deliberately go about this business of getting ideas for yourself. If you are under 40 you will probably need to do so anyway. But youth, with most of its life ahead, has more opportunity for spontaneous events. There are incentives sprinkled all along the way if one knows how to make use of them.

Maybe we have said enough to have something upon which to start. Here is your year—what shall you do with it? But you have got to get that idea. Heaven knows, our lives are prosaic enough. Ask yourself the following questions:

What do I want to do in life?

What things have I put off doing?

What am I most dissatisfied about?

If I had the money, what would I do first? Second? Third?

How could I get some of the money in the world? At least a little more?

Obviously I do not propose to tell you *what* to do. That is not possible—my prescription would probably not fit *you*. But those questions are designed to keep you thinking until we have gone a little further. Ideas may not take shape at all in the lines we have mentioned, but it will help to have your mind receptive toward certain things.

And remember—unless all signs fail, ideas are going to come to you, often in unexpected places and unexpected ways—even while in bed. You will learn why as you go along. Keep your little notebook with you. Your book is an important thing.

[32]

{3

Where Do Ideas Come From?

Everyone, it seems, talks about ideas, but few people are specific about how to get them. A person starting to teach creative thinking encounters blank looks on the faces of his students during the first few weeks. To them it seems strange that anyone should tamper with "those mysterious laws of creation" and assume that they, just students, could have ideas. After a few weeks, the blank looks fade and, by the end of the semester, the students usually have a surprisingly large number of workable ideas.

Just what is an idea? An idea, our old friend the dictionary says, is "any product of mental apprehension or activity." Or it may be "a conception" or "a notion." Or a "purpose or plan." Or "a mental image." Or a "standard of excellence" or an "ideal."

But I think I like my own definition better. "An idea is

the mental spark that ignites the gas and starts our idea-mobile going." And, once started, it may carry us in many directions and to many as yet unknown places. Ideas produce events that change ourselves and the world as well.

Everything that man does starts with an idea, or a succession of ideas. The steam engine was an idea. The automobile was an idea—many ideas. The flying machine was an idea. Great books and paintings are ideas. Everything is an idea down to the tube of tooth paste or the wrapper on a candy bar.

This matter of creation or invention—for it is really one and the same process—is fundamental to life. Men and women are measured in the world not by their drudgery but by their ideas, particularly when these ideas are translated into action.

To start off, we are going to take a trip and see what we shall see. Many highly successful businessmen take trips with the sole purpose of gathering ideas in their respective fields. But we are not committing ourselves to one field. We are going to take a look here, there, and everywhere.

"What gorgeous buildings!" I exclaimed one day as I was walking over the campus of the University of Colorado at Boulder. The buildings seemed to violate the rules of traditional college architecture. They were unsymmetrical in line. They sloped at various heights and angles. They were built of local sandstone which varied in color from yellow to reddish-purple.

But now we come to the significant point. Where did the style of those red-tiled buildings originate? They came from the barns and houses of rural Italy. Charles Zeller Klauder, the Philadelphia architect, had planned, like so many architects of university buildings, to follow the traditional Gothic style, but he became so impressed with the site and the materials lying right at hand on university property that he evolved this "new idea" in architecture. And yet we know where it came from.

One day I visited the Opportunity School in Denver. Here was a wonderful institution which had for its fundamental idea that of teaching people what they wanted to learn rather than teaching them what others thought they should learn. It was Emily Griffith's brilliant idea. She saw that there were thousands of people in a big city who wanted to know specific matters that were of great importance to them.

For example, one day a man came to the school with a desire for a strange bit of schooling. It seems that an important company was considering him for advancement. But the new position would require that he entertain people socially at dinner. He had never done anything of that sort. Would the school help him to learn? And it was a pressing problem indeed, for the next evening the owner of the company and his wife were inviting him to dinner at a hotel to see how he would get on. Emily Griffith and one of her assistants delighted in that kind of problem. They arranged a table just the way it would be in a big hotel, and together they sat down and went through the imaginary meal from soup to mints. They even rehearsed a line of small talk that would be suitable for the occasion.

I know what you, the reader, are thinking: Did the man get the job? Yes, he passed the "examination" the next night, and the owner of the company promoted him.

In Santa Fe there is an art museum, known somewhat

[35]

formally as the Museum of New Mexico Art Gallery. It was built half by public subscription and half by the state. It is the architectural composite of six Spanish missions. Its towers and balcony were inspired by the church at Acoma while the missions in the pueblos of San Felipe, Cochití, Laguna, Santa Ana, and Pecos contributed details. But here we are not concerned with the architecture, interesting as it is and quite as distinctive as that of the buildings of the University of Colorado. There is something else that originally represented almost a radical departure in art museums. Instead of trying to cover the art of the world or of America, it confined itself to art of the southwest or art produced in the southwest. What a sensible idea! All over America were museums longingly seeking the old masters but without resources to procure great pictures. But here was an institution developing the art resources of its own region.

I was seeing Hollywood. Hollywood has the reputation of being "colossal, stupendous, and gigantic." One may expect to see anything from restaurants that resemble gigantic hats (The Brown Derby) to moving picture palaces that derive their style and architecture from foreign lands (Grauman's Chinese Theater). Or, as Frank J. Taylor once remarked, "Igloos for ice cream, doghouses for hot dogs, giant oranges for orange juice, and tepees for real estate." Of course, it is easier to put across the bizarre in Hollywood than in almost any other part of the United States.

But I am not dealing in this book primarily with the colossal or stupendous. I am interested in everyday reality. And looking about, what do we see? Here is a manufacturer of costume jewelry. Most of the old-style and antique jewelry worn by movie actresses comes from his workshop. But why should not other people like this type of jewelry? So he adapted it to modern wear and sold thousands of dollars worth through department stores.

In both Colorado and California, a few years ago, I saw the beginnings of a word. "Hotel" when applied to tourist camps became "motel" and "autel." But "motel" won out, and tourist camps throughout America become "motels" rather than "autels."

In Arizona, wise promoters saw what the climate did for "T.B." and what "T.B." did in bringing visitors and residents to their country. They asked what other diseases might be similarly benefited. Arthritis was one answer and became the foundation for doubling the tourist business. A little observation showed that the sun might not be the great liability to the southwest that so many people pictured. Why, it could really be an asset! And so the sun country was born.

In Dallas, the Marcus brothers, sensing the profitable accomplishments of luxury stores in big eastern cities, adapted the idea to Dallas. "We always buy more than we plan; we seem to sell it," Stanley Marcus told me. You can buy a $25,000 fur coat there. Neiman-Marcus now does business even with people who live in the big eastern cities.

In Oklahoma City, "chicken in the rough," which means eating chicken with the fingers in the good old southern way, was transported to the restaurant (with even a little pail of water in which to wash the fingers). Several other new ideas were used in this restaurant development, and royalties were charged scores of restaurants using them elsewhere.

[37]

In Wichita lived a composer, Thurlow Lieurance, who developed a successful piece of music, "By the Waters of Minnetonka," from an Indian melody. Many famous ideas in the arts have come from primitive sources.

We ride on streamlined trains and in streamlined automobiles, both of them borrowed from the airplane. Once the airplane borrowed from the railroad train and the automobile. Now, strangely enough, it is repaying that debt to other forms of locomotion by furnishing them with ideas.

All right, what about it? What we have seen is what you, too, have seen all about you. Interesting new things arising in business, design, education, music—things that may mean money in the pocket or what is more consequential, a better and more enjoyable world.

And all of them coming out of something else. More specifically: A famous designer of women's clothes raids the Brooklyn Museum for "new creations." In one recent year her creation of a new woman's suit jacket came from a man's hunting jacket shown in the museum. A "domino coat," which possessed the doubtful asset of making a woman appear as if she were leaving a tent, was the old pyramid coat of 1866. One year the designer managed to get ideas for fifteen dresses out of the museum—not a bad record! Do not think that she simply copies these things. She adapts them to modern use.

The Costume Institute of the Metropolitan Museum of Art featured a "Casablanca to Calcutta" exhibition. There you saw an exhibit of fabrics that had been based on source material in the museum. Side by side you could see the original from which the adaptation had been made and also the new design itself. A peacock and floral design embroidered on an Indian skirt became part of a design for several different fabrics by Hafner. Wesley Simpson had noticed a head of Krishna designed for a mural in the palace of the Maharajah of Jaipur. Just one item there, the tear drop pearls, furnished the foundation for a green rayon dress with black scallops and white tear drops.

There are today great machines for mathematical computation. They grew out of the idea of the machines used for automatic telephone operation. Officials of the Bell telephone system were not satisfied with the scope of the calculating machines used for their mathematical computations and decided to build their own—using the same principles they were using for automatic switching.

In California the Mediterranean style of architecture is developing so fast that standing on the deck of a steamer, one might well imagine himself on the Italian Riviera. That architecture is particularly suited to sunny climates.

In the prosaic field of cooking a professional caterer makes his beets, carrots, sweet potatoes, and radishes so attractive that they might be taken for exotic flowers. An artist not in paints and crayon, but in ordinary food.

Now! What have we learned so far?

Each new development or bit of creation starts from something else. It does not come out of a blue sky. You make use of that which has already entered the mind, or that which you cause to enter the mind. That is the real reason, the great reason for accumulating knowledge.

In order to test this principle, carefully analyze ideas that came to you suddenly—those that you can recall—and determine what was really their foundation. Talk with your acquaintances who have created something new—whether it be invention, new ways of selling goods, writing, music, anything—and ask them how it came about. Don't their experiences agree with what we have said?

If you happened to be Louisiana-born and were landing on the beaches during World War II, you would not have been mystified at the strange landing craft carrying you to the shore. "I remember these," you would be saying to yourself; "we used something like them to get the lumber out of the shallow bayous and rivers." And that would true, for that is where Andrew Higgins got the idea and first used it, and where he developed those craft.

But if you had been a Dutchman in Louisiana and had run across one of those boats getting out the lumber, you might have said to yourself: "I remember boats like this used on the flooded lands in Holland. There was a tunnel under the stern and we put the propeller there." And that country is where Andrew Higgins' idea came from originally. Of course there were many, many improvements and many, many new developments, but it was there the idea started.

And where did Walt Disney get his Mickey Mouse? The mouse introduced himself to Walt Disney, all unannounced, and the two became such good friends out there in Kansas City that Mickey, originally known as Mortimer, used to play around the drawing board while Walt Disney was trying his hand at localized Kansas City movie cartoons.

He had been working with Oswald the Rabbit for a New York distributor, but there was a disagreement and Disney was out in the cold for taking such pains as to suggest improvements. He wondered what he could start with that would be bright and new. There was Mickey Mouse occupying a place in Disney's brain. "A mouse," he exclaimed, "that's it." And so Mickey became immortal.

Occasionally you may run across individuals who do not know how they did it or who like to make great mysteries of their accomplishments, but most people who really make a business of creating things know the process they went through.

You have a question here. You say to me: "You have made things very simple. But everything cannot be so simple. Many things are very complex."

"Yes," I answer. "That is true." Most pieces of creation as they stand today do not represent just one jump but many successive jumps. For example, hundreds and thousands of scientists and inventors each did at least one bit in the field of electricity. And sometimes that one bit was sufficient to get their names in the encyclopedia. Civilization represents millions of pieces of creation, each put there by someone or other. Ideas are piled one on top of the other and thereby make history.

Suppose that you were sitting in a group of seven or eight persons, three of them physicists and the others ordinary intelligent laymen. And the conversation turned upon the wonders of electricity—the light, the telephone, the electric train, radio and television, not to mention the scores of doo-dads that naturally delight the woman in the kitchen and the man in the office.

And you might say solemnly: "What a debt all of us owe to Edison! He invented everything in electricity, didn't he?"

"Not everything. Bell gave us the telephone, didn't he?" another layman would say.

[41]

"Well, don't you think we should mention Marconi?" a third would ask. "Didn't he invent the wireless?"

The scientists would look at you in tolerant amusement.

"Of course, of course," the first scientist might say, "those men did some things, but don't you think the real credit goes back to Michael Faraday and Joseph Henry who, in 1831, found that electricity could be generated from magnetism?"

"My dear fellow," the second scientist might interject. "Yes, they did a few things, but don't you think it was really that Frenchman, Arago, and that Englishman, Humphry Davy, who did the job ten years before? Remember they discovered that an electric current circulating around a bar of iron turns the bar into a magnet."

The third scientist would put on his most controversial expression. "Yes, yes, some credit maybe, but don't you recognize that it was really Oersted in Denmark back in 1819 who made the great discovery that a bar magnet, freely movable, sets itself at right angles to a nearby wire conducting electricity?"

Probably you have heard many set-tos such as this and enjoyed them. But the imaginary conversation does illustrate the point. The great men were great enough, but they started with something else. Their achievements all depended on something that had gone before.

Many, many men had something to do with the steamboat, not just Fulton alone. Many men had a great deal to do with the telegraph, not just Morse. And many men had a great deal to do with the automobile, not just Henry Ford. But I would not be surprised if half of the children in a grade school would pipe up "Henry Ford" if you asked them: "Who invented the automobile?"

Creation is everywhere about you, but, as we have pointed out in this chapter, each thing is built upon something else. Our next problem, then, is in determining how these successive matters of creation arise, what the process is, and how we both consciously and unconsciously may make use of it.

4

Ideas Sparkle Everywhere

THERE ARE TWO PATHS to successful learning or accomplishment. One is inspiration. The other is technique. Many books that have dealt with creative thinking have been purely inspirational. "Jim Jones did it, so can you," is the theme. Naturally, if you have enough energy and enthusiasm, you will accomplish something. But that is only part of the whole. The book that you are now reading emphasizes techniques and demonstrates those that are fundamental and successful.

How do *you* go about the task of securing ideas?

Playing with ideas without knowing the process is something like building an automobile by trial and error. You may finally get it done, but it would be much easier if you knew how in the beginning.

Possibly you are a businessman. I don't know what you

are selling. Maybe it is insurance, maybe it is annuities, maybe it is real estate, maybe books. But the point is that you are not selling things as rapidly as you would like. Looking through some magazines, you run across that advertisement of the Alexander Hamilton Institute which has for its basic theme, "the years that the locust hath eaten."

"It must be a good advertisement," you say to yourself, "because it has been used so often." Remember the theme? The young fellow who keeps putting off improving himself until it suddenly dawns on him that it is too late? Finally, in mature life, he is still sitting on the high stool in the back office, while his boyhood chum who busied himself is now at the mahogany desk. A great basic advertising theme, and a true one, that might be applied to insurance or annuities, or house and home, or books, or religion. Maybe you have tried such an advertisement, using the basic principle, and you have found the replies coming in. I did so once myself, and the advertisement drew the greatest number of replies ever received by a prominent corporation on a project of the kind.

You are a nurseryman. You have been paying a visit to New York City and have been walking up Fifth Avenue and down Park Avenue. You have been observing the efforts to glamorize those streets. Sometimes this is accomplished by magnificent buildings; sometimes also, as on Park Avenue, by islands of green grass; and sometimes by such things as the flower beds in Rockefeller Center.

But you can't help comparing things with old Puffle Avenue in your home town, a street that is declining from its one-time residential elegance and acquiring stores and office buildings. It is now in that between-stage—not quite residential and not quite business. But it is a principal artery into the city and ought to look better.

Big, fine office buildings right now are out of the question for Puffle Avenue—that takes huge money. Then you suddenly think of those flower beds at Rockefeller Center. And then you think a little more—what kind of flowers? Because you are in the nursery business, you want to sell everbearing roses. No one is allowed to park on Puffle Avenue; yet the street is very wide. You have a sudden inspiration. Why not plant everbearing roses all along both sides of the street? You can urge all property owners to plant roses in their yards. Instead of Puffle Avenue, you plan to call this the Avenue of the Roses.

You may have to do some promotional work with the chamber of commerce or the women's club in order to centralize the effort. But I can picture most property owners as only too willing to assist with the program since it would enhance the prestige of the street and raise the selling price of their properties.

And, don't forget. If you are a nurseryman in that town you would surely not lose anything by selling a hundred thousand or so rose bushes. Even if you are just an ordinary member of Rotary or Kiwanis, you would have done your good turn for the year.

You own a small department or general store. You have thought longingly of the reputations of Marshall Field and Wanamaker. You would like to give your own store national fame and reputation, but you are not sure just how you can do it. You have not the capital to start a great store, and you fear that your community might not support such a store anyway.

[46]

But many times you have walked up and down the streets of the large cities peeking in the store windows. Christmas displays are lavish indeed. You decorate your own store at holiday time, and you see how your decorations could be improved. Of course! Of course! But you are not sure you could afford high-priced window decorators. Suddenly, however, a moderately bright idea pops into your head. That morning you had been attending a baking contest with scores of women all baking cakes at the same time. At the moment you seem to be contest conscious. Why not have a women's club, church, or school competition in your community for the decoration of a Christmas window? The different organizations or schools would submit their ideas, and then you would choose the plan of one, furnish the material, and let it do the decorating.

Good advertising for your store, and people will all look at that window. Local interest might make up for lavishness. But the idea lacks somewhat of achieving your first aim— a national reputation. Anyway you put the idea down in your notebook. May be worth trying sometime.

So you keep browsing around. Another thing in the big city stores intrigues you—those luxurious Christmas baskets full of all sorts of delicacies. You price them, but you are not sure people in your town would pay those prices. And you could hardly afford to plan such a variety of baskets. But anyway you jot down the idea in your notebook, and on your way home you consider the possibilities.

Suddenly you think you have it! You are going to take the Christmas basket out of the price class, make it a bargain item and then merchandise it. You are not going to have a great number of elaborate holiday baskets. You are going to have just one basket and that is to be the most wonderful basket full of good things that ever sold for $4.95 or whatever price you are going to put upon it. At the start you are not going to try to make money on it. It is going to be a special treat for your community. Profits can wait for the longer future when you have the idea established and everything can be bought at rock bottom price.

You start out examining baskets. Maybe at the start you have only a market basket. But you are going to color it and attach a big ribbon bow. Or possibly you will choose one of the Mexican baskets. Maybe you will see interesting possibilities in those unusual, finely woven baskets that the Indians make in San Blas on the west coast of Mexico.

What are you going to put into the basket? You seek out those mammoth walnuts, twice the size of ordinary walnuts. You get some of those rare bits of chocolate from Holland or Switzerland and some of those unusual sweets from Portugal or Spain. You wonder what might be developed that would be a little unusual in your own community. You know your state is famous for hogs. Large hams would be too expensive, but there are the small picnic hams. You put your store kitchen on the job of finding a new and enticing way of baking them. Maybe honey from your state, or nuts, or some unusual fruit preserve will add just the right touch in baking the ham.

The more you play with your basic idea, the more ideas occur to you. It becomes a delightful hobby the year through just planning the items you will include. You find many food producers only too willing to have new delicacies introduced to the public via your basket and glad to give you a special deal. Even some of the great chinaware kilns of the world might include an unusual piece or some silversmith a bit of unusual silver.

As the years progress I can picture your Christmas basket becoming one of the famous institutions not just of your community but even of the nation, as it is shipped here and there by customers. The first thing you know you are in the mail order business in a big way and on the road to that coveted national reputation.

You are a musician. You visit the Indian reservation. You hear a few strains of a plaintive melody. And you say, "Ah, just the foundation for a sad little waltz!" And people say, "Yes, he's a composer."

You are one of countless unknown artists, doing well enough but not making much of a name, and you begin studying cartoons. "You know, I believe I have an idea," you exclaim. "I'm going to make my paintings just a bit like cartoons in their irony and humor." The critics may proclaim you a genius, but you know where your idea came from. Incidentally, I can say that Thomas Benton did that very thing, and the critics did pronounce him a genius.

You run a small restaurant. What a time you are having over the price of meat! What could you give your patrons that would be distinctive and attractive, good tasting and yet moderate in price? You know how tired your patrons must be of "chopped beef" on the lower-priced dinner. So you go out on a browsing tour of the big chain store that has everything in meat just laid out for your inspection.

One item intrigues you, those rib steaks that can be had for much less than the price of other steak. They are really good meat, just the same as rib roast for which you ask such a big price. But, in your small restaurant, rib roast stands quite a while, gets cold and dry, and loses its luscious taste. There is generally waste. The low price of rib steaks appeals to you, but most people associate them with cheap steak. You turn the whole thing over in your mind. You have it! You are going to serve individually roasted ribs of beef piping hot from your kitchen ovens. And with your hot ovens, you know you can do it while the folks are taking care of their soup and salad. Or, if you have older ovens, you can keep a few pieces roasting gradually. You know you can put it on a lower-priced dinner because you can pick out those slices of beef beforehand and hold each to a required size and price. And you don't have to roast a lot of them to be held for a future meal. People can have the meat rare, medium, or well done. You are going to glamorize rib steak by calling it "Individually Roasted Ribs of Beef."

Of course, if you are a housewife, there would be nothing to prevent your using the same plan. There must be thousands of housewives who would like to serve rib roasts but do not feel they can afford to pay four or five dollars with "only two or three in the family." You, too, would be glamorizing rib steak.

We have been creating things right before your eyes. But let us for a moment consider what has really been happening.

Creation generally consists in the *shifting of attributes from one thing to another.* In other words, we give the *thing* with which we are working some new *quality* or *characteristic* or *attribute* heretofore applied to something else. Remember how we discovered a great basic theme in the Alexander Hamilton advertisement—years passing and nothing done—and reached over and applied it to our project of selling insurance, or annuities, or books.

On your trip to New York you acquired one attribute out of Rockefeller Center—the flower beds. Oh, of course there were many other attributes that enhanced Fifth Avenue, but you chose that one as the most desirable and workable—a very important consideration—for enhancing the prestige of Puffle Avenue. You also made another important change: you had rose beds all along the way on Puffle Avenue instead of in just one spot.

The department store owner took a highly specialized item, the Christmas basket, and set out to mass-produce and merchandise it—a new attribute. It was the same idea that Henry Ford had used in popularizing the automobile. There are many items in all stores that have never been exploited. The Christmas basket idea might suggest others.

As a musician, you adopted the theme of the Indian song for your waltz or light opera number. As a painter, you used the attribute of the cartoon. A sculptor might have done the same in his field.

As a restaurant keeper, you took your rib steak and, instead of broiling it, you reached over to the rib roast idea and created the idea of roasting it. Or you might have started with the rib roast idea and reached over and created the idea of roasting it in *individual* pieces to order—the attribute heretofore applied to steak. Of course, it is not so important where you start in this business as where you end up. Our minds, fortunately, are more concerned with the end of a process than the beginning.

But, regardless of how we have looked at the matter, you are going to have to admit that we are now confronted with some highly successful products. We have resultful advertising or promotion for our own business venture; we have turned poor old Puffle Avenue into an Avenue of the Roses; we have a wonderful low-priced Christmas basket; we have a restaurant with a successful roast beef idea; we have some "talked about" art; we have some new music. All in all, it is not a bad haul for a few days' fishing.

What Is This Process?

Perhaps you do not catch the full import of what we have been doing. Let us analyze it a bit further. Being original is simply reaching over and shifting attributes in what is before you.

In the first place, this is not imitation. If you were making no changes at all, it would be imitation pure and simple. Of course, you might say that transferring an entire process bodily to our own instead of another person's management would be creative in that we changed the place of manufacture. But the output of the creation would, from the world's point of view, be simply the same old thing. Being an imitator is not particularly creditable nor does the world give you much credit. There are wonderful paintings scattered about Europe so marvellously executed that experts can hardly tell them from the originals. But they are only copies, and, as soon as the fact is known, the price falls to almost nothing. Hundreds of "doodads" are being sold at negligible prices in dime and department stores because they are only imitations of the original. But they are sold at a low price only because the original patents or copyrights have run out or possibly they were not fully protected in the beginning.

Remember that the creative process is *not* generally a matter of combination as some old-style psychologists have vaguely asserted. Combination is just putting two or more things together. Of course, looking backward, you may say that shifting attributes or characteristics is a form of combination, but such views are psychological hindsight after the creation has already been accomplished. Making combinations does not generally permit you to move forward because you do not know what to combine in the first place. It leads nowhere except as an occasional accident. You might combine garbage cans and sofas, or ink and ice cream sodas, or sidewalks and bureau drawers and have nothing worth while at all. Only occasionally does playing with combinations yield anything.

Nor does the world proceed on the principle of combination. Rather it grows in an orderly fashion along the lines of constant adaptation.

But the process we have outlined involves three steps. We look at one thing (process or idea). From this we select or think of one unusual or strong quality or attribute. Then *we apply that attribute to something else.* And we have a creation.

Now, of course, we may like what we already have very much. Instead of giving away one of its attributes to something else, we bring to it an attribute from some other thing. We may substitute this attribute for some attribute already in existence or just add it on. This is, however, just another way of looking at the same old process.

You are always measuring the things before you in terms

of their attributes or characteristics or qualities. Rightly handled, this process leads to specific and desirable results.

Getting Started

It is surprising indeed that a great number of people just wait at the idea station and never board a creative train of thought. But all about them are thought starters. Obviously, these thought starters do not tell you in so many words, "Here is the beginning of an idea that if pursued further—often much further—will be a whale of an idea for your own company." Newspapers and magazines, not to mention your own observation along the street, give you hundreds of tidbits with which to start. Different minds see different possibilities, but many minds see nothing.

For instance, hidden away in about 50 words at the bottom of a newspaper column, I read the interesting statement that 300 women workers from General Electric's plant at Fort Wayne plan to tour six European countries in the summer. Their weekly wage has been averaging fifty-seven dollars, but they will pay their own way. Now, sitting there in your commuter's train, you probably think, "How nice it is for those girls!" and that is all there is to your thought. The lecturer across the aisle is going to pound the speaker's desk and use it as an example of what the American way of life can do for people. The stenographer, however, in the next seat comes close to an adaptation, "Wonder what I could save up for?"

But the sales manager who cultivates the mental attitude of thousands of Sallies and Johns in this world immediately sees something of great import to hundreds of companies that ought to be seeing it too. It is the fact that people in modest walks of life are seeking luxury that they can afford. The airlines began to nibble at this possibility a few years ago with their special trips to Europe, but it suggests prodigious possibilities for all sorts of hotels, railroads, and steamship companies, not to mention theaters, concert halls, restaurants, fur coat manufacturers, etc., etc.

It is not our purpose here to inquire into the origin of the idea, but others have sensed the huge untapped market for low-cost volume merchandising in the field of luxury. Many a white elephant in business life has been transformed by the application of an idea. I am thinking of one of the luxury hotels near Biloxi. It was picked up at a bargain price by an enterprising man from Florida. The supply of available millionaires was running low, but there were thousands of people in the country who would enjoy a luxury vacation "if only it didn't cost so much." Now you can have a fine room and bath for less than you would pay in most commercial hotels, and in the great dining room you can eat the old millionaire's dinner for a little over two dollars. The grapevine reports that the hotel is now on a good financial basis.

Ideas sparkle everywhere. Watch for them, particularly in your own mind.

And so we close the chapter. I have tried to keep it simple. But I know that a great fundamental question lurks in your mind. And right there, in the title of the next chapter, you'll find the answer, waiting for you.

5

How to Find the Attributes That Become Ideas

No amount of physical labor, doorbell ringing, or expenditure of time can substitute for the absence of creative thinking, which often represents the difference between failure and success in any venture," says Dr. Norman Vincent Peale, a great preacher and writer.

From now on we are prospectors looking here, there, and everywhere for those precious ideas. Our search has narrowed down, and we find ourselves seeking attributes or characteristics on which to start to build ideas.

And naturally you ask me: "Just what am I to look for?" That is a good question.

You may, of course, work right within your own field of employment or activity where ideas are needed. We have also suggested that you should begin to think in terms of your great ambitions, your desires, and your plans for the future. If these things have been implanted in your mind, it is probable that your activity will gravitate in such directions.

But remember that a miner is not too much disappointed if he strikes uranium instead of gold, or copper instead of silver. Nor does the owner of a farm feel too badly when he finds an oil well replacing his potato patch.

In the idea business the world is your oyster, and you may look around wherever you like. The Elgin Watch Company, for example, has announced the creation of a commercial development department as its first step in a long-range program to diversify its manufacturing and sales operations. It plans to make exhaustive studies aimed at selecting new business fields that the company might explore advantageously. The Parker Pen Company now makes cigarette lighters. General Motors and Chrysler have for years been making products that are clearly outside the field of automobiles. You are going to be in good company when you look around for different things to create.

As you look around, recall the formula for the process of creating ideas we discussed in the last chapter. You remember that what you must find is an attribute you can take from one thing or idea and apply to another.

It is obvious, of course, that your attribute has relationship to the thing that you are considering at the moment. It would be impossible to take as an attribute of an oil well its wintergreen flavor, or of an electric lamp the fact that you use a match to light it. The oil well and the electric globe do not have those attributes. The attribute that you first single out is always part of the thing.

Everything has a very large number of attributes. Not just one or two or a dozen, but usually hundreds of possible attributes that we may single out, if we want to dig deeply enough.

For example, let us consider a house. Here are some of its characteristics or attributes: colonial style; eight rooms; shingle roof; good rental location; frame construction; cheap to build; white paint; blue roof; two baths; built-in kitchen cabinet; hardwood floors; bright, large-figure wallpaper; sunken garden in backyard.

Now I might enumerate many other attributes that belong to this house. You may take your choice of the attributes, but they are likely to be the ones that you personally favor. In creation, your selection of attributes has everything to do with the finished product.

Or take the automobile. To find the attributes of cars you have only to read the magazine advertisements: styling; quick pick-up; color; power; economy; leather upholstery; low repair bills; brakes; power steering; electric windows; blowout-proof tires.

Now, of course, there is really no limit to the number of attributes we could discover if we look hard enough. We might even go so far as to set down the design of a hub cap.

But a significant fact is that most of these desirable attributes are set out in the form of what they mean to us as owners rather than as technical designers.

That immediately brings us to the important question: *What attribute shall we look for?*

The Controlling Factors

What factors generally control our choice of attributes? Most of the time we work with them unconsciously, but it will help to put them down. There are five dominant ones:

Money-making and commercial possibilities.
Labor-saving possibilities.
Preservation and well-being of ourselves and others.
Beauty and appeal to the senses.
The current of the world's thinking.

Whatever dominant attributes we see in things are generally in terms of one or more of these factors. You do not have to stay within their scope; it is simply that doing so may lead you to ideas more easily carried out later on.

When we think of these controlling factors we should think in terms of the other fellow more often than of ourselves. If he makes money by using our product, we'll make some, too. And we should think of saving labor for the other man, not just ourselves.

Down in Florida I know two men who are starting a paper mill. And what do they plan to use for material? Rags? No. Wood pulp? No. They are planning to use sawgrass, which grows wild in the Everglades country. In fact, so abundant is it that the yearly yield may run as high as 50 tons an acre. It takes only four tons of grass to make a ton of paper. And why are they in the business? Because they believe they can save newsprint publishers at least 20 per cent on their paper bills. And they hope to make some money, too.

The Dearborn Motors Corporation, a Ford subsidiary, is turning out low-priced cotton harvesters which sell for around $1,200 and can be attached to a tractor. Big, full-size machines have sold for $8,000 to $12,000, but most cotton farmers do not have enough acreage to warrant such a machine. A small machine will save the low-acreage cotton grower twenty-five to forty-five dollars a bale over hand picking.

Naturally, if you save labor, you also make money. The Illinois Central Railroad and the Omar bakeries have begun to handle flour in covered hopper cars. The advantage? It eliminates packaging, weighing, and handling of the ordinary 100-pound sacks of flour. The cars are sealed against dust and have smooth inside surfaces. A vacuum process simply sucks the flour from the cars.

The Kroehler Manufacturing Company is reaching over and adapting the automobile manufacturers' assembly-line techniques and applying them to furniture. At Naperville, Illinois, the parts are being turned out mechanically on a moving assembly line. The company expects to save labor by producing parts mechanically and, then, by maintaining assembly plants in various parts of the country, to save tremendous shipping expense. It is estimated that 75 per cent more freight can be loaded into a car or truck when furniture is shipped in pieces rather than put together. The net result will be lower competitive prices for the consumer.

We all like to be lazy, and that, too, accounts for the second factor. Of course, it is many times related to our first factor, but that is simply because labor-saving devices sell well, or cut down the cost of making other devices. All sorts of household gadgets, foods, machines, and ways of doing things have been invented solely because they save labor.

How lazy can we get? There is apparently no limit to the possibilities. The other day, a neighbor's four-year-old boy, seeing me walk to the corner drug store, admonished, "Why don't you take the car?"

I received a strange and interesting letter from the manager of a fashionable apartment house in Florida. The letter said that it was difficult to rent the luxurious third-floor apartments with a beautiful view to *young* people. *Young people*, mind you! They would no longer walk up two flights of stairs. Is that a tipoff to an approaching real estate situation that will suddenly depreciate apartment houses more than two stories in height with no elevators? And yet the old-timers walked up a hill, climbed the front steps, and often labored up three flights without a murmur. In Florida today, most of the new, smaller apartment houses are no more than two stories. Will the second story finally go and everyone refuse to live on any floor but the first? A trust company in Lincoln, Nebraska, finds a tendency that way.

Will college departments that have classes on the third floor no longer have students unless the students are required to take these courses? Will Spanish be favored over French because it is on the second instead of the third floor, and will great crowds of students be taking Psychology 181 because it is a first-floor subject? And will professors on the fourth floor in some old-time institution demand compensatory remuneration for extra effort required? Laziness can make a variety of changes.

When you arrive at the matter of the preservation and well-being of ourselves and others, you consider something that is born in us. Here we include everything from vitamin pills to sanitariums, from schools to churches, from the Marines to the Air Force, from city to national governments. Anything that keeps us alive and up and coming, and that prevents us sliding downhill physically, socially, or financially is popular with us. We want it.

When Frank Gerber died, Rev. C. John Westhof, pastor of the First Presbyterian Church of Tulsa, declared that the babies of America had lost a great friend and benefactor. And what had Gerber done? He had built a $50,000,000 business out of an idea that was literally thrust upon him. A doctor had recommended strained foods for one of his grandchildren. What a job that was, cooking small amounts of vegetables and mashing and straining them each day! Frank Gerber wondered why he could not do it on a bigger scale and lined the grocers' shelves with "Gerber's baby foods."

You can think of hundreds of items that belong in this class. The Abbott Laboratories have just put on the market a plasticized skin cream that protects against all sorts of skin irritants. The Minnesota Mining and Manufacturing Company now has a Scotch tape that sticks six times tighter than the old tape. And, down in Texas, the lonesome cowboy need be lonesome no longer for the Leddy Boot and Saddle Shop in San Angelo will sell him a saddle with a built-in radio.

That last item brings us to another interesting factor: beauty and appeal to the senses. Beauty or appeal to our senses is flexible. The first three factors are almost universal in making an appeal to people, but this fourth factor makes an appeal in different ways to different people. It depends a great deal on their past experience and their developed likes and dislikes. Some people desire to strengthen their self-esteem; maybe they want European automobiles. Others like things that appeal to their sense of taste—chocolates, for instance. Women wear perfume; men do not. Some of us like to mix with other people; some prefer solitude. Some like the outdoors and beautiful sunsets; others like the theater. So this is not a universal set factor. It is highly variable.

But it is powerful. It is usually glamor in action. And I mean by this not just the glamor of the Paris gown or the ballroom but the superlative everywhere. The Brenner Desk Company of Newark, New Jersey, will, for instance, sell the tired businessman a $7,000 desk. He just pushes a button and the panels fly open. There is an electric shaver in one compartment, a radio in another, a bar in a third. Maybe some would classify this desk as a labor-saving asset, but I put it down as an appeal to vanity.

This factor pervades almost everything. The Santa Fe Railroad's Super Chief boasts a luxurious private dining room, the Turquoise Room; the Milwaukee, observing the popularity of dome cars for travel, introduces a full-length dome car so that more people may enjoy more beautiful scenery; the Chesapeake and Ohio has only all-room sleeping cars because all people seemingly want such luxury.

Down in San Antonio, Cosimo Lucchese turns out luxury cowboy boots at prices as high as $200 a pair. The automobile manufacturers offer color and more color. As I write, there are 228 different tints of automobiles. Blues and greens are the most popular, while sombre black has dropped 50 per cent in popularity.

This beauty and appeal to the senses can be big business, too.

Neison Harris, of St. Paul, Minnesota, bought the small Noma company which made hair-waving equipment for beauty shops. He had acquired some knowledge of chemical cold waves and began to develop home-waving kits so that every woman might achieve hair beauty in her own home. You might raise your eyebrows at the sight of a Yale graduate giving practical demonstrations—for that was what he did—but Yale is proud that it has an alumnus who could sell a business for many millions a few years later.

Finally, we take a look at that matter of consciously or unconsciously favoring attributes that are within the current of the world's thinking. This thinking may be strange at times, but we are more prone to swim with it than against it. Our minds gravitate easily to ideas within the world's thinking, and at the same time those ideas succeed more readily because they are in that field. Of course you do not have to stay within the current. It may simply make things a bit easier if you do so.

I sat next to Rev. J. R. Perkins, pastor of a Congregational church in Council Bluffs, Iowa, at a luncheon. Twenty-five years before, he told me, he had written a book, but the publishers would have none of it, saying that its day had gone by. But, with more confidence than most of us would have felt, he had put the manuscript carefully away. At the time of my talk with him, he had already taken the typewritten pages from his trunk, revised them, and the book was being made ready to appear as *The Emperor's Physician*, later to sell hundreds of thousands of copies. The vogue for religious novels had returned, piloted by Lloyd Douglas.

That feeling for religious fiction had probably existed for a long time; Lloyd Douglas pushed it back into the public consciousness.

Keeping within the current of the world's thinking is not as difficult or imposing as it sounds because the thinking of the average person—your own thinking—is usually bounded by the world's thinking at the moment. The reason is that it requires less effort. From the idea creator's point of view, there is accordingly less sales resistance.

Remember what President Eisenhower did to the hat business? By wearing a hat on every occasion, Eisenhower stood as a public reprimand to the hatless faddists of a few years before. More than that, Eisenhower wore a homburg, and soon the well-dressed man wore a homburg. And yet, only a few years before, a big clothing store in Lincoln, Nebraska, sold out its stock of homburgs for one dollar each because people would not buy them. No wonder James B. Lee, president of the Frank H. Lee Hat Company, termed Eisenhower "the nation's greatest hat salesman."

And remember Queen Elizabeth's Coronation? Everything in England became "Coronation." We must report one failure, for not all ideas succeed. *The Wall Street Journal* told how Derek Traylen, a sausage maker of Cambridge, in a great burst of patriotism turned out sausages in three different colors: red, white, and blue. But alas, they would not sell. Blue sausages did not seem to fit the occasion.

Fads and fashions arise because of the propensity to select a dominant attribute at the moment, particularly if it seems financially profitable. A publisher, for instance, observes the success of long novels and soon has his authors turning out long novels. A few gardeners have rock gardens, and soon everyone is seeing what he can do with a rock garden. Platform rockers come into vogue, and shortly every furniture maker is using that basic idea. A few women are inveigled into hats that are not really hats, and soon all milliners are following that style. "Our competitor down the street was advertising ice cream colors," a former student who was writing advertising copy for a Chicago department store told me, "so I just thought up sugar bonbon shades."

Sumner Blossom, editor of the *American Magazine,* conducted a department called, "Why Don't They?" He said that very frequently several hundred people expressed exactly the same idea, each thinking that it was wholly original. Whenever an American ship was torpedoed during the war, suggestions for antisubmarine devices would pour into Washington. When European cities were bombed, ideas for air-raid shelters would spring up.

You have probably noticed something about these factors. They are closely related. They come together many times. In selecting some attribute you may do so because it will save you labor, or enhance your well-being, or because it appeals to your senses. You want widespread adoption of your idea, and that often carries us right back to the question of commercial possibilities and whether or not it is within the world's thought. In other words, if you seek general acceptance of your creative work, you cannot always please just yourself, particularly if you are a little unusual. There is something to be said for those who bowl the world over and force it to accept what they like, but right here we shall pass that over temporarily. You may, of course, create such things. I simply point out the difficulty.

How It Works out

Now back to the house. You say:

"I'm going to have a house with that style of architecture."

"I'm going to have an extra shower bath, one of those glass showers with red walls."

"I'm sure I want a built-in kitchen cabinet like that one."

"When I build, I'm going to build in this location. I know it's the fashionable part of town, and I can readily sell again."

What have we? Any one of those things put into your house or another house will be, from the standpoint of the house, a bit of creation, for you have changed the house.

You may call them imitation, but is using that style of architecture in the house imitation any more than using the Italian type in the Colorado university? You have made a change, and, in its most elementary form, that is creation.

Some of the changes you made were for financial reasons or prospects. For example, you built your house in that location because you thought you could sell it more easily later on.

But some of your house creations appealed to labor saving, particularly that type of kitchen cupboard. Perhaps the sunken garden idea appealed to your sense of well-being—you could work there evenings—as well as to your esthetic sense. That blue trim appealed to your sense of beauty, and you decided to adopt it for your place.

But maybe you refused to adopt one of the attributes of the house—Colonial style—because you felt that a modern or ranch-type house would be more in keeping with current trends.

This house has been rather a routine affair. It has been an ordinary house with plenty of ordinary attributes. The great problem for the past decade has been to find means and methods to better the house, to make it more livable, and, most important, to produce it at low cost. Building costs have been too high for the ordinary pocketbook.

Suppose we were to transport ourselves to one of the developments of Levitt & Sons at Levittown, Pennsylvania, or Levittown, Long Island. What might we find there? The average builder would see so many things it would make his eyes bulge. He would find a complete heating plant that takes up little more space than a small kitchen table. He would find the heating pipes embedded in the floors. He would find a light bamboo screen hung from a ceiling track as a closet door. He would find the kitchen moved to the front of the house and the living room to the rear.

Most significant of all, he would find mass production. Prefabricated houses are not new. But the Levitts prefabricate on the spot instead of having heavy, bulky sections of the house done at the factory and moved to the site. The assembly line process is used, but instead of the framework of the house coming to the builder on a belt, as in a factory, the worker moves from house to house to do his individual stint.

Now, those who have traveled about recognize that these things are not entirely new. They were not pulled out of a magic hat. In Korea, it has been traditional to heat the floors of houses from underneath. I have seen many American houses with the living room at the rear. Manufacturers have considered the possibilities of small heating boilers—remember the small steam plants on the old-time steam automobiles? I have seen mass production of houses. What happened was that the Levitts picked up and transferred to their jobs the most successful attributes they had noted not only in building but in other fields.

The Levitts have emphasized landscaping of properties in other developments. Why? Well, the father of the firm, Abraham Levitt, saw that landscaping would to a great degree offset the depreciation that customarily takes place. What an idea that is for all of us who desire to rejuvenate old properties! I recall Florida hotels that are *really* old. But their grounds are so beautifully landscaped that they are comfortable places indeed. And they can maintain very substantial rates. Walk down the streets of your own city, and for a minute see all the possibilities in taking the age off old flats, hotels, and private homes by the addition of rose-bordered lawns, rare shrubs, window boxes.

Sometimes you will see something that, at first glance, you do not feel belongs in this pattern of creative thinking. But, on second thought, it is simply a neat part of the same old pattern. For instance, someone tells you of the trick of making things smaller. So you build a bedside or vacation-type radio, or you make a small-size tube of tooth paste or ointment to be sold at the variety store. Someone tells you to make your product twice as big. And you design the giant size of your cosmetic, or you institute a two-for-one sale. Someone tells you to try plastics. Today they have plastic plumbing. You can take scores of meaningful adjectives and apply them to your product but, after all, it is only changing the attribute.

Let us call these attributes that we choose *point of observation*. Often they are very obvious. The adaptations made in many advertising and merchandising campaigns are of the obvious sort. The man who sees the success of the orange juice habit and supplants it at the breakfast table with grapefruit or pineapple or prune juice has engaged in only modest creation, although it may be highly profitable for his industry. He has simply asked himself, "What is the idea in this orange juice?" And he answers, "Using it as a pleasant health beverage." And that quality or attribute is perfectly adaptable to other things. Merchandising and advertising men are always thinking in these terms. "Dated coffee" might be shifted to hundreds of other things, such as candy, bread, fresh vegetables, etc.

Discovering this dominant quality or attribute that you are going to apply to something else is not such a formidable task. In advertising and merchandising, it fairly shouts at you. It is the quality that makes the product sell. It is usually right there for all to see.

Merchandising is full of ideas and yet receptive to any additional number of them. Department stores, for example, have long used hour sales to stimulate activity when it might otherwise lag. That idea might readily be adapted to restaurants and barber shops.

Even single ideas may accomplish a great deal. Great restaurants and hotels have made reputations on certain things. Parkerhouse rolls and porterhouse steak were named after hotels. I recall a Spokane hotel for its strawberry waffles, a Tokyo club for the way it displayed its food, a Colorado dining car for its mountain trout, a Denver restaurant for its distinctive ice cream desserts. It will be of great value for you to play with this principle for a while even though its full import will not come to you for a few chapters as yet.

Have you been keeping that little notebook I suggested earlier? How much have you in it?

Remember, an idea a day might well keep the bill collector away. Deposit your ideas in your book as you would money in your bank.

6

The Great Art of Observation

THE OTHER DAY I tossed a squirrel a mammoth walnut. To him, the idea of a walnut was a great event. He
grabbed that nut, and off he went across the housetops. But
soon he was back, the nut still in his mouth. Then up a high
tree and back again. That nut so thrilled him that he was
showing his discovery to all the neighboring squirrels, or
perhaps he did not know where he could safely hide such
a treasure.

I tossed another squirrel a big English walnut. It bumped
against him, and he smelled it. Then he hopped off and went
on digging up his little acorns.

Some of us are acorn diggers and do not know an English
walnut idea when it actually bumps into us. Some of us go
through life and see so little.

But others have visions.

Remember? Fulton was an artist, but he built a steamboat. Morse was a portrait painter, but he developed the telegraph. Eli Whitney was a school teacher, but he turned out the cotton gin. Machine guns, smokeless powder, and rifled cannon were invented by civilians.

It is an astonishing fact that many men have stepped outside their chosen fields and have made important inventions. They saw things that even men brought up in a certain line of work had never observed.

Observation is the key that unlocks the door of creation, and there are many keys to observation itself. Sometimes observation seems to have a combination lock.

But some people have a hard enough time discovering really dominant points or attributes, let alone those obscure ones that would lead a man like Sperry to build great stabilizers for ships from his original observation of a top spinning.

What Is Observation?

What makes us observant?

Profitable observation is generally the detection of differences. It is seeing the significant, important and out of the ordinary.

Why did this tree live, and why did those near it die? Why does the paint on this house last so well? Why is there so much demand for these apartments while those across the street are vacant? Why does that little chain of stores make so much money? Why does this bread taste so good? How could a publisher turn out a book like that for twenty-five cents? Why did the experiment come out differently from the way we expected? What is the nature of that new material?

When you know the answers to questions such as these, you are started on the road to adapting the successful and desirable idea to your own needs. In the course of time you will not only have ideas that may pay immediate dividends, but you will have accumulated a tremendous background on which the mind may draw frequently.

Most education has been defective here. Most memories are cluttered with trivialities. Schools and colleges are to blame for not training us better to pick out the really important instead of the insignificant things. Our memories should become reservoirs of great adaptations on which we may draw.

Our minds will function readily enough in pulling out the right adaptation if we have always followed the questioning attitude. The subconscious mind will have less difficulty with this process of adaptation, if it has previously understood the process. Creation is, as we have pointed out, very systematic, but the difficulty has been that we have generally expected our minds to work at the matter without ourselves understanding it.

Creation consists of observation and then the adaptation of the attribute observed. Roentgen happened to pass his hand between one of his vacuum tubes and a screen. He saw the bones of his hand revealed. Right there was the first fluoroscopic examination. By making an adaptation, using a plate, instead of a screen, the image of the bones of the hand was permanently preserved.

The use of X-ray as a means of killing cancer cells was based on another observation. Some of the early experimenters with X-rays saw the devastating effect of X-ray burns and reasoned that if the rays could destroy normal cells so easily, what might they not do to cancer cells? There was another observation in connection with this—that X-rays had their most deadly effect on cells that rapidly reproduced themselves, such as cancer cells. One adaptation after another!

Observation is no magic power; it is simply finding things out. You have to take yourself in hand and make yourself do it. You open your senses to the things about you. See what you see, smell what you smell, taste what you taste, hear what you hear, feel what you feel. Using our eyes, noses, tongues, ears, and fingers is not something strange. The difficulty is that we have allowed ourselves to become so absorbed in routine matters that we seldom use our senses.

You have to train yourself to examine what is before you. First of all, begin now. Eat your bread and butter, and really taste it. Really listen to the music on that radio program. Feel the delicate softness of that milkweed fluff (some people did that in World War II and found it made an excellent substitute for kapok). Smell the aroma in that coffee.

Guide Posts to Observation

Here are some exercises that will greatly aid your powers of observation:

1. Take a walk, slowly, looking at buildings, trees, flowers, automobiles, everything you run across. In each case, pick out the distinctive features that make the particular object interesting and valuable. Could the attribute be applied elsewhere?

2. Examine the outside of a public building. How many evidences of adaptation in architecture and materials do you find?

3. Examine a toy. Why do people like it? Could any of its attributes find a place in another toy? Or could you change the present toy?

4. Choose the field in which you are most interested and make some observations there.

If you are in business, seek to find out the underlying reasons for the most successful business of that kind in your community. If you are interested in mechanics or chemistry, browse through some books on those subjects and see what practical applications or adaptations you can make from fundamental principles contained therein. If you are interested in writing, examine two best-selling novels and determine what makes them successful. Or go through a current magazine, asking yourself what caused the editor to select the articles and stories in it. If you are a musician, examine some classical material and determine in your own mind if there are possible adaptations to popular music. If you are interested in art, examine some modern pieces and ascertain what departure from generally accepted practices you can find. If your own work is languishing, see if you can not bring some distinctive and original touch to it.

With your eyes, begin to see things. Sight, of course, offers us the most profitable field of observation. Every time you take a walk, or go to a movie, or eat a meal, make a practice of finding one rather dominant idea. As we have indicated, the quickest and most profitable way of doing this is simply to pick out something that seems marvellously successful

[76]

and find out what makes it so. Or, sometimes pick out something that is a "flop," and find out why it is that way.

Great corporations make a regular practice of sending skilled investigators around ringing doorbells and asking questions with no other thought in mind than to find the answer as to why some products or ideas are successful or unsuccessful. Probably some have called upon you, with no greater aim than to ask your opinion of some stories in a magazine or why you dislike a certain breakfast food.

William M. Jeffers, president of the Union Pacific Railroad, had a nationwide survey conducted to find out the desires of railway coach passengers. That resulted in the inauguration of low cost, fast transcontinental passenger service with trains offering low-priced meals, more space, free pillows, better reading lights, and a graduate nurse in attendance.

For a long time a famous airplane designer has been studying the fly, because, as he says, the fly carries with it the future of airplanes. The fly has everything—speed, lightness, durability, easy steering, and economy. It makes upside-down landings on a ceiling with ease. In fact, a good part of the fly's design has already been adapted in that, like the fly, only those parts of the modern airplane necessary to flight are carried outside. Remember the old-style airplanes? Everything was patched on here and there to encumber rather than aid flight.

The Value of Observation

Few things will bring you greater reward, both financial and personal, than using this power of observation. Herbert

Fleishhacker, out on the road selling paper boxes, heard one day that a large tract of lumber land could be purchased cheaply from the Southern Pacific. He organized his own syndicate to secure the property. The resultant profits netted the Fleishhacker brothers $300,000 and gave them their big start.

Dr. Preston C. Iverson, working in the plastic surgery department of Walter Reed Hospital, made an important observation, followed it up, and created a new and highly successful method of eliminating the wound tattoos—bits of imbedded powder and dirt—on the faces of soldiers and the ravages of acne and other diseases on the faces of countless civilians.

Doctor Iverson's observation was this. He had long practiced skin grafting. Probably most doctors would have thought about skin grafting and more skin grafting, but Doctor Iverson began to think about something else. The interesting thing to him was how well the place from which the skin had been taken regenerated new skin. This operation is done so skillfully that only half of the thickness of skin is actually removed.

And he got to wondering if maybe the unsightly places on people's faces, such as the wound tattoos, might not be cleared up entirely if just the upper layer of skin were removed. He wondered how deep most of these blemishes actually were, and he found that generally they were no deeper than half the thickness of the skin. If perhaps that amount of skin were removed, the blemishes would disappear too. The question naturally arose as to the process best adapted to removing this skin. The ordinary methods would not work so easily since the face was not flat. The

[78]

actual thickness of the skin to be removed with the blemishes would have to be controlled. And then Doctor Iverson thought of sandpaper. How simple that seemed to be! Sanding off people's faces instead of boards. And there was one of the most valuable discoveries in the field of plastic surgery.

It is conceivable, of course, that another individual might have developed the idea directly of adapting sandpaper to skin instead of boards. Doctor Iverson's thinking came the long way around. But maybe *you* can discover new uses for sandpaper.

A professor from the United States one day observed the low cost of producing sterling silver articles in Mexico. But most of the silverware was inclined to be a little rough and was usually imitations of old standard patterns. But he said, "I'm going to open a silver shop and make new modern designs that are more in keeping with what my artisans can do." He made a great success.

You observe in an out-of-the-way corner of Mexico some highly original and bright-colored baskets being sold at very low prices. Why would they not have a wonderful sale in the United States? Your idea is simply to import them and make a profit.

You are an advertising man and you observe that your competitor is causing his advertising to be read because it is so humorous. Or you observe the success of comic-strip characters, and you bring them to advertising. You observe Elsie the Cow and Elmer the Bull, and you decide on Joedy the Horse. This sort of simple adaptation goes on all about you.

A man from the United States had lost a great deal of money and was looking for ways to recoup his fortune. In

Canada, he saw a new kind of oat growing in an experimental field. "Why not bring it to the United States?" he asked himself. He did so and sold large amounts for seed.

A man picked up a hairpin on the street, turned it over in his mind, and out came the paper clip.

One envies our soldiers and sailors scattered all over the world their opportunity of observing so much. They are familiar with things from our country that we might adapt to other countries, and they see strange things from other countries that we might adapt to our own. The whole world of the trader opens before them. And the return to business of World War II veterans did give new impetus to foreign trade.

Maybe you are interested in selling unusual things. Thousands of new and fascinating articles are sold by direct mail. You see advertisements of them in *The New York Times Magazine* and other publications. Think of that advertising genius, Webb Young, and his necktie business in New Mexico. He arrived in that business by observation. He became interested in the lore of the Southwest and the problems of the Indians. He wanted to help them. From his past advertising experience and his new knowledge of the folk arts of New Mexico came the idea of selling handwoven ties by direct mail. He has sold several million dollars worth of ties. The poor Indian weavers saw their weekly income more than tripled.

This might lead you to consider selling another type of necktie or an entirely different type of product by mail. You might change the attribute and, instead of neckties from New Mexican wool, sell neckties made from those rare pieces of old brocade from the Orient. You could make the suggestion in your advertising that personal pride demands that a man wear something rare and costly about his neck! Women wear pearls and diamonds, you know. What about intriguing men into the adventure of something very rare in neckties for their throats? A New York shop recently advertised mink bow ties. Or you might change the thing and sell unusual writing paper made in France. Or you might sell new and delicious foods.

A significant thought here is that if you have something very special to sell, you will probably get a little extra price and that extra price makes possible paying for the advertising. Taking your product out of the ordinary run of competition is important if that can be done. A textile man and I were discussing in Tokyo the marketing of silk from Japan. Our own government, which had counted on silk to help pay the costs of occupation, had missed the boat and failed to sell stocks of silk when prices were good. Silk prices in America were beginning to tumble. Both of us were in agreement that selling silk on a cheap competitive basis with rayon would be difficult. Rather it had to be sold on the basis of being a luxury product. It will be interesting to see what creative ideas for the merchandising of silk are originated. One innovation might be the introduction into America of the huge silk handkerchiefs in which a Japanese woman wraps all of her parcels, ties the knot, and carries the whole thing easily along the street.

Many people work in shops and factories where inventive skill is at a premium. "What shall we look for?" they ask. Here is an answer in the interesting "think list" used by the General Motors Corporation:

1. Can some machine be used to do a better or faster job?
2. Can the fixture now in use be improved?
3. Can slides, conveyors, or stock handling be added or changed in position or sequence to improve the operation?
4. Can a special tool be used to combine the operation?
5. Can the quality of the part be improved by changing the sequence of the operation?
6. Can a cheaper material be substituted satisfactorily for that now in use?
7. Can the material used be cut or trimmed differently for greater economy or efficiency?
8. Can the operation be made safer?
9. Can forms be eliminated?
10. Can established procedures be simplified?

Thousands of potential ideas exist everywhere. "We have a fellow in our Elmira plant who told us we were wasting a lot of time and money on a certain operation," R. J. Roach, general manager of one of the divisions of Remington Rand, remarked. "It was in the manufacture of type bars for typewriters. That's the thing on the machine that comes up and hits the paper when you press the key. His suggestion asked: 'What's the need of using a straightening operation after blanking these things out of a sheet? After they have been burred and cleaned we form them a certain way, so what's the use of pounding them out flat?'

"What was the use? Well, many times management doesn't have the answer to a question like that. And when we don't have the answer, it is entirely possible that it means a money leak in production. We like suggestions like that. The suggester got $1500 for that idea."

No one need feel that opportunities are limited to invention or those creative arts such as literature, painting, and music. As we shall see later, there are great opportunities for simply doing good in the world. And do not forget agriculture, which has been remade by science and observation. One day Colonel E. Parmalee Prentice was showing me about his country place at Williamstown, Massachusetts. There the short grass was being mowed and put in bags for animal feeding later. "Grain," the colonel called it. Then I remembered that my saddle horse had always spent his leisure hours munching the short grass and letting the long grass severely alone. He always refused to mow the part of the lawn that needed mowing. But it had never occurred to me that, from the animal's point of view, the short grass had very desirable qualities. It took Colonel Prentice to put the principle into application, just as he had done with other ideas in the agricultural field.

Do not be discouraged if your powers of observation are not 100 per cent effective. If they are 50, 75, or even 10 per cent effective, you may be doing very well by yourself and by the world. A century ago, a Swiss college professor combined cellulose with nitric acid and obtained nitrocellulose. He predicted that it would replace gunpowder but, as Williams Haynes aptly remarked: "He caught no vision of bright-colored plastics, or luscious rayons, or tough, quick drying lacquers, or transparent wrappings. Yet all these, and other new products, too, lay in the future of cellulose." But Christian Friedrich Schönbein had accomplished enough to have his name in the chemistry books.

An investor raised the question: "Here I've got plenty of money, and things are going down. Where do I invest it? I seem to be out of luck just sitting around." But she did not see that the greatest opportunity possible was waiting for her. If prices of things decreased one-half, she had done the same thing as doubling her money, for, without being invested at all, it would double in purchasing power.

If you don't turn things over in your mind, you may fail to see their significance. One afternoon I was talking with E. Haldeman-Julius, who had conceived and successfully carried out the idea of selling millions of copies of little "blue books" at a nickel apiece in lots of twenty. You saw his full-page advertisements everywhere. "But it was a strange mistake I made one day in appraising another man's idea," he remarked. "DeWitt Wallace, getting his *Reader's Digest* going, had sent me a copy. The funny thing was that, looking through it, I could not see the great possibilities. But look where he went with his idea."

The power of observation is one of man's most valuable possessions. Everywhere there are things worth seeing and thinking about. But as we are beginning to learn in this chapter it is not only necessary to observe but to turn the observations over in your mind and make something new out of them.

{7

Creation Is a Continuous Process

Everything seems to have been done. I just don't see how anything else can be invented because the U. S. Patent Office is running over with inventions."

This was not written yesterday or even in this century. Instead the words were penned more than 100 years ago. Much more astonishing, they were the words of the chief of the United States Patent Office as he resigned in 1833. He didn't think there was anything left to be done.

Since that time more than 2,500,000 inventions have been perfected, not to mention many million more ideas that were not or could not be patented, but nevertheless left some imprint upon all of us.

Creation is infinite. It will never stop, neither in time nor space. Its possibilities are absolutely limitless. It will go on and on and always at a faster rate. The more things that are created, the more things there will be to create. Creation becomes an inexhaustible reservoir. Partly this is because, as the lady of the house says, "The more furniture I buy, the more things I have to buy to go with it." But there is, of course, a much deeper reason. Creation keeps going faster and faster because there are more things on which to build. And each attribute of each thing is susceptible to new applications in scores or hundreds of directions. The cave man needed everything, but he had created few things of his own with which to begin. The man of a hundred years hence will have so many things that he will hardly know where to start.

Let us hear William Osler speaking: "All scientific truth is conditioned by the state of knowledge at the time of its announcement. Sir William Perkin and the chemists made Koch possible; Pasteur gave the conditions that produced Lister; Davy and others furnished the preliminaries for anesthesia. Everywhere . . . one event following the other in orderly sequence."

Remember, too, that nothing will ever be the same as the thing made just before it, because no matter how hard we may try there will always be some variation.

In a house, the possibilities of change are thousands times thousands. We might theoretically be so perfect in imitation that we would have everything just the same in a second house except the exact positions of the nails. If we varied each of ten nails successively in relation to the changing positions of ten other nails, we would have ten times ten times ten *ad infinitum.* Finally we would be up in the millions, and all we would have done was to change a few nail holes. We could not duplicate a house no matter how hard we might try.

Creation spreads out in all directions. So far we have worked with just simple basic qualities, and those are usually the important factors, at least with which to start. But any piece of creation radiates outward and multiplies itself until perhaps the original thing cannot be identified.

There are two reasons why you often do not discern bits of creation in their essential simple quality. In the first place, the mind carries out this process wholly unknown to you as you work with it. The mind suddenly changes the attribute or applies it to something else.

The other reason is that most creations are the result of dozens, even hundreds of changes that, put together successively, represent the finished product of your thought.

What we are engaged in here is conscious direction of our creation. So far we have generally considered changing only one attribute of a thing. Why? Because the mind in conscious direction seems to have difficulty in doing more than one job at a time. The exception is when two or more attributes are considered together as a unit. For instance, white typewriter paper, or selling things by mail. Each of these, of course, has many different attributes, but the mind has grown accustomed to considering them as units by themselves. It is just the same as in writing or speaking. Then we usually think in terms of groups of words, rather than one by one. We do not have to think separately of "typewriter paper" and "white" because usually it is "white typewriter paper." The mind can catch the entire idea at once. That, of course, saves our minds a tremendous amount of work as we go through life.

[87]

The second reason we generally work with one basic attribute is because usually one basic attribute initiates or starts our creation. We see the significant attribute first. But it is advisable to understand where other attributes fit in.

Let us go back to our house again. Suppose we change the Colonial style to English style, the frame construction to brick, the shingle roof to slate, the blue roof to a gray one, the sunken garden to a formal English garden, and so on. Suddenly we have planned an entirely different type of house by changing many attributes. In fact, we begin to see hundreds of possibilities in changing attributes here and there. That is what architects are constantly doing, reaching here for a plan of outside architecture, there for a modern heating plant.

We have seen this before, but what we are noticing here is that we have changed only one basic attribute at a time. However, within each attribute are other attributes. There are many different kinds of paint, many different kinds of brick, many different flowers for the garden.

What is the meaning of this to you? It is that successive adaptations may be necessary in completing your invention. There are hundreds of inventive possibilities.

Let us take a very simple, elementary example, one where we consider two attributes at the start. We consider a table. It is *wooden* and has *four legs*. We change it to a table with *five legs*. Then we decide to make it a *metal* rather than a *wooden* table.

But there is nothing very startling in our idea as yet. So we ask ourselves, "What is taking the place of metal and wood in beautiful ornamental work?" "Plastics," we answer and decide to try them. We change *wooden* to *plastic*. We seem to have created in our minds a *five-legged plastic* table. Then instead of a *table* we wonder what other furniture might be made from plastics. A *bedstead* occurs to us. We drop off one of the five legs, because a fifth leg hardly seems suitable for a bedstead.

Now we are happy, and off we go into the matter of checking on plastics. They are beautiful; so we consult with one of our chemistry friends. "The idea is all right," he says, "but the difficulty is in finding cheap plastics that are strong enough."

What shall we do now? Shall we work on locating plastics that might be both cheap and strong? Shall we strengthen plastics? Both ideas might be promising, but the latter idea might be too difficult for us. So we do some more thinking. Suddenly we say to ourselves, "Why not combine metal or wood and plastics?" And our chemistry friend tells us, "You have something there." So we bring out a bedstead with beautiful plastic panels at head and foot.

Thinking that originally started with a wooden table has now, by means of repeated adaptation, led us into plastic panels. And we say to ourselves, "Where else might we use plastic panels?" After considering a number of places we exclaim, "For walls!" The pressed wood now used for paneling comes close to the idea, but perhaps we shall have plastic walls with considerable ornamentation and design.

You might have chosen other adaptations—there were scores of possibilities. There are many pathways to creation, and you may choose any one of them. One man does one thing one way and another does it a different way. One difficulty with the assimilation of purely how-to knowledge in high school or college is that different methods will be in vogue when you are out in the world.

Dr. Herman Schneider, the famed engineering dean at the University of Cincinnati, told me one day what confronted him on graduation. "We had been taught how to build wooden bridges in our engineering course," he remarked, "but when I got out I found they were no longer building wooden bridges." So, when Schneider became dean, he had students working in industry as part of their course.

A young man who had been a successful copy editor on one large newspaper found himself employed by another paper. He wrote to me in distress one day, "You know, they find fault with the way I do so many things."

"Never mind," I wrote back. "That's just their way of doing things."

While nearly all corporations like to get ideas, they may at a particular time be emphasizing certain other ideas. Everything must contribute to those special ideas. But even this kind of situation offers the beginner an opening. It was W. L. Fletcher, Boston personnel consultant, who always showed how to turn prospective defeat into victory. When the young fellow is sitting there, quaking in his boots because he is being told he has had no experience, all he has to do is to say something like this: "Well, now, maybe that's an asset, since your company is a leader in its field and I am not impeded in working for you by preconceived notions acquired with less efficient organizations." The prospective employer may well burst with pride when he hears that.

We must remember that great projects require thousands of ideas all working toward an end. "History of carrier aircraft development over the past 15 years shows that an average of three to five years is required to develop a basic design using available scientific knowledge," remarked John F. Floberg, former Assistant Secretary of the Navy for Air. "As design complexity increases, this time span of aircraft growth approaches even longer periods. Dependence upon supporting research areas previously unexplored may also increase design time. Although prototype flights indicate a successful design, service evaluation may reveal deficiencies requiring another one or two years before quantity production begins. . . . In the final analysis, it may be said that approximately five to seven years are required after design inception before an aircraft can be expected to be operational in service use. A number of fighter aircraft are known to have taken over seven years to reach production stages."

That is why many corporations work years ahead on certain products not knowing whether or not they will turn out successfully. They are engaged in a long battle with ideas as ammunition.

Flights of Genius

"But," you say to me, "Many pieces of creation are not like those you have been talking about. I tell you, some people have flights of genius."

If you aspire to those very obscure adaptations that will rock the world, that will make people think you are profound, you will reach over and bring an attribute out of an entirely new field and apply it to your own activity or find an obscure thing for the old attribute.

Theoretically, we can, of course, substitute anything in

[91]

adaptation. It is always possible to step into very bizarre creations. That happens when we change a common quality into a most unusual one as an insane person might do. Suppose that instead of a four-legged table, we suddenly decide to have a table with twenty legs. Maybe we are not yet crazy; there might really be a very ornate table with twenty legs. But change the thing, a table, to a horse. We now have a horse with twenty legs.

What have we done? In the first place, we have jumped to something that has no connection with a table—a horse. Of course, we do not make horses, except in a picture, but a horse with twenty legs even in a picture would be something of an oddity. It is true that an insane person might readily believe that he saw such a horse. Artists often seek the impossible. One modern Italian artist does paint horses with many legs in an attempt to get across the idea of movement.

Bizarre cases simply demonstrate that people in their right minds are logical, almost too logical in fact. Their creations proceed only along the lines of close association. When we make these unassociated jumps in our adaptations, we produce all sorts of nightmarish things. Once in a while even one of these may turn out better than we would think and come into general favor. It has happened often in musical composition.

It may do that logical mind of yours good to make some bizarre creations, as we did in the case of the twenty-legged horse, where you simply put down anything. Change anything to anything and keep on going. William Seabrook, the author, and I spent an evening at it and found it more fun than crossword puzzles.

Or take a joke and play with its component parts a while,

changing the characters, situations, main point. The main point is probably the thing, and the characters and situations the attributes. This is the process that joke writers pursue, but unfortunately they often do not go far enough in changing the characters, situations, and main points. The result is that their jokes seem imitations and not new creations.

There is a great deal to be said for unusual creations. Nature itself is, of course, infinite. It is full of strange and unknown things. So it is not too radical a procedure for people themselves to create strange things.

Art goes off on limitless tangents. Japanese art went in for symbolism, and designs became metaphors. Perhaps you have walked through Japanese museums and have pondered over such matters, as did A. Davison Ficke, when he saw women drawn as if they were lilies, men as if they were tempests, mountains as if they were towering giants.

Japanese artists in the old tradition forget all about shadows, which they regard simply as illusions, unworthy of art. Distance was indicated by placing the object higher in the picture. Their pictures were flat and were meant to be that way. It is conceivable, of course, that an American artist might adapt some of these ideas to his work and be hailed as "a new arrival."

Grant Wood, the Iowa artist, got the idea for his stark paintings from the Flemish primitives of Europe. Art must often make use of obscure adaptations. It is always a question just how far one may profitably go with unusual adaptations. Corot learned to depart from the accepted pattern of art, giving to his pictures a misty, dreamy quality, which was in its way a step toward modernism but not such a bold step as to keep him from reaching popular acclaim during his lifetime. But he did not sell his first picture until after he was 50 years old.

Some impressionists achieved brilliancy by decomposing colors. They placed component colors side by side on the canvas, allowing the spectator's eye to reassemble them. Blue and green in tiny streaks appeared brilliant green at a distance instead of dull green as when mixed beforehand. Whistler, Manet, Degas, and, later, Van Gogh and Gauguin absorbed Oriental design in their art.

Obscure attributes are not so easily discovered, but if we look here and there at what is before us we may discover them. This is where past knowledge and memory enter into the situation.

But what makes you remember? Largely observation. If you do not observe and notice closely, you do not remember a person or thing.

There is an interesting point about this profound thinking. Many people make discoveries but do not create things, for they do not change anything except theoretical knowledge. Many people knew the principles on which the wireless telegraph is based and the principles underlying the photoelectric cell, but did nothing about them. It had long been observed that gas is cooled when released through a narrow opening, but the iceless refrigerator was long in coming.

What is the suggestion to you? Simply this. If you aspire to those great fundamental things, study books of chemistry, physics, and the other sciences. Learn what the principles are, and then make your applications. One of the very great philosophers one day remarked to me that regardless of the contributions of others to the fundamental principles contained in my teaching of creative thinking, my name would go down as the one who had brought them to practical application.

The use of obscure or little known principles may result in great things or perhaps only gadgets. One man devised a profitable toy in the shape of a miniature bulldog that came out of the doghouse when you clapped your hands.

Few of us are going to make use of very obscure adaptations. We are going to do the more obvious thing, and the more obvious thing will probably make more money. The more obscure adaptation may finally win great acclaim, but it will be harder to impress the world with its importance. Perhaps Frank Floyd Wright, the architect, is an example of this. He departed from tradition, not occasionally but nearly always. It took time for him to achieve recognition and see the adoption of his ideas.

Industry is not apt to have so many flights of genius since it hardly dares get too far off the beaten track. At least it has to keep one foot on the track. People often present a united front against ideas that seem too revolutionary. Remember that once bath tubs were regarded as forerunners of ill health and that railroads were supposed to be carrying people to perdition.

Several years ago, a representative of the Los Angeles Chamber of Commerce, Miss Genevieve Staley, was trying to get the New York stores to buy and promote Hollywood fashions. But the stores would have none of them. "They're too bizarre out there in Hollywood," Miss Staley was told. "New Yorkers won't stand for Hollywood fashions." The Californian was undaunted and possessed the true California creative touch. She made an adaptation, "Let's call them California fashions." The stores were willing to accept them under that name, and California fashions were on their way to success.

What This Is Not—a Brief Review

We should understand quite clearly what this technique is not as well as what it is:

1. First, our basic process is not just inspiration except in so far as inspiration means that the body and mind are active—in good trim, so to speak—and able to work as quickly and readily at creating as they would work quickly and readily at anything else.

2. The method of creation is not just a matter of combination, as some have implied. You do not pick up an armful of different things and throw them together in that rather vague way that some have called creation. *Each time we take a step we do it by changing an attribute or a quality of something, or else by applying that same quality or attribute to some other thing.* The pattern of great pieces of creation may involve hundreds of successive changes. The creative step is the same, but it is repeated many times with many variations. If you doubt this, examine any notable building and count the adaptations. In any piece of music you will find scores and scores of these adaptations. The mind takes just one step at a time, and it may do this very rapidly. It may consider several changes at one time, but only when they can be considered as a unit, as for example, the general style or architecture of a house. Usually there is just the one dominant change with which you start.

3. An important point, which we again emphasize, is that we do not generally see these attributes or things as simple

[96]

abstracts. When we reach out and pick up some quality or attribute, it is always in relation to some particular thing. Even when we think of such a highly abstract quality as softness, we usually think of it as the dominant quality of a pillow, a piece of velvet, or something else with which we may be familiar.

4. In making an adaptation, another consideration arises, one that we have already mentioned, but which we again emphasize. When we change our attribute, we usually change it to something that stands in close association to it. In the development of the commercial possibilities of fruit juice as a breakfast drink, we proceeded from orange juice to grapefruit juice to other juices. When we change the thing and apply our same attribute to it, we generally pick a thing that is closely related to the other. We sell men's shirts by mail so why not sell men's socks by mail? That means that creation is generally a progressive and orderly procedure.

5. Creation is not stealing another's work. Of course, the line between new creation and plagiarism is often a very fine one, because the change may be slight. Any patent attorney can tell you how slight the change and how narrow the interpretation may be in determining that something is really new. Then, as we have pointed out, a "new" thing usually involves not one but dozens of adaptations before it is finally complete. Often the original idea with which we began is no longer seen at all in the complete product. Any man who just sits down and copies something is plain dumb. The process of creation is so simple and so easy, when one understands it, that even the best of things is usually susceptible of improvement.

How to Search for the Unknown

THERE ARE MANY PEOPLE and many companies that know they want to do something, but they have not the slightest idea of what it is. If they constantly worked forward and kept a notebook full of ideas for the future, the BIG idea would already be at hand.

Suppose they have not been doing that and have to start from the beginning. Many companies that had expanded during World War II found themselves in that kind of situation at the end of the war. They will find themselves again and again in such predicaments whenever business becomes slack, whenever their products become "dated," whenever they must expand to hold unit costs down. What are they to do with themselves and with their plants?

The Doepke Manufacturing Company of Rossmoyne, Ohio, found its machine shop busy enough during the war years, but, as the war ended, the question arose, "What shall we do for a regular business?" To use their factory, they had to have something that could be stamped, pressed, and embossed in métal. So they looked around. One day, Fred Doepke brought in his child's toy water truck for repair. It was made of wood, but Charles and Fred Doepke asked themselves, "Why not of metal?" They had noticed that many such toys were rather fragile, and they determined to make larger models that would withstand the most destructive child. Their miniature concrete mixer actually makes concrete, to the consternation of parents. They get substantial prices, from twelve to twenty dollars apiece for models of everything from bulldozers to fire trucks.

Another company, faced with the problem of finding a new product at the end of World War II, considered making lawnmowers. Studies were made of all the other lawnmower companies. How were they getting on? How did they advertise and market lawnmowers? The company contemplating the lawnmower business asked consumers whether or not they liked the mower they used. What influenced the consumer to buy a particular kind of mower in the first place? Now that he had it, was there anything the matter with it? What features would he like in a new one? What would he be willing to pay for a tiptop machine? Then the question arose as to the actual construction of a lawnmower. Metals and plastics were considered. Engineers determined the exact angle of the handle where the mower would work most easily. The kind of bearings was chosen. Next the mower was styled to make it attractive. And finally a few models were tested on consumers to ascertain how they liked the new product. Then they felt they were ready to make a successful mower.

But suppose you know what you want or what someone else expects you to create. Suppose you receive this kind of order: "Will you please provide the following items for a television production of *The Sleeping Beauty:* one frog to talk, wink, go to sleep, and catch flies; one handkerchief to speak and show pain; one tulip to open and reveal a baby; three flies for frog to catch; six little spiders spinning webs on six little practical spinning wheels; one goose to play solitaire; one growing rose hedge; one deer, one horse, and assorted bugs, rabbits, butterflies, squirrels, etc."

Quite an order, isn't it? Of course, no one would send you one like it, but it illustrates the point that sometimes we have to work backwards to get what we want.

Many people arrive only half way on the road to creation and yet think that they have created something. Instead of actually creating something, they have found only *a need for something to be created.* For instance, they want a glossy but nonslippery bathtub; they want a foolproof automobile; they want a certain cure for cancer. Noble as this activity of the mind is, it is not yet creation for it has not changed anything. More than that, these people have not yet found a way of doing so. They have accomplished something in observation, but observation of pressing needs is not always a great accomplishment.

But "from a slightly different angle," remarks L. S. Hardland of the National Inventors Council, "there is the tendency of the man with an idea to feel that that idea constitutes an invention when in actuality all he is presenting is a broad, general concept. He fails to realize that the idea, the suggestion, the concept may be the simultaneous brain child of a great many people but that the man who produces the invention is the man who is capable of producing the concept and working out the developmental details."

This indicates our second approach to the matter of creation. Up to now, we have generally suggested that we start with a known thing, select one of its attributes, usually the dominant one, change it, and so proceed directly to something new, or apply the attribute to another thing. This method is the one that most minds follow, the prescription that most of us follow unconsciously. It is to proceed from a known to an unknown thing. We get a new thing in a hurry.

What we set out to do now is harder. We start from a thing as yet unknown and proceed to its discovery. Here you cannot expect to achieve results as quickly. You are not certain what you are to find, but you do make use of the same principles. What you are to find is something, which, by changing one of its attributes or by changing the thing and keeping the attributes or by making successive changes, you may adapt to solving your problem.

You perceive the general difficulty here. At first, everything seems unknown. What we are looking for we see only in dim, hazy outline. The old thing and the change we are to make to produce the new are as yet unknown or uncomprehended by us. It might almost be said that we are starting with three unknowns. What we are seeking, we know better than anything else, but as we have said, only in dim, hazy outline.

You readily see that we have quite an undertaking ahead of us. How are we to proceed? It is in this type of creation that we may draw upon past knowledge, where we must make use of the knowledge and background that we have accumulated. Henry Ford, for instance, got the planetary transmission of the Model T from an old Swiss watch and the differential gear from an old tractor.

Reverend Willis Dick, a Marietta, Ohio, minister, found his task much simpler. He wanted a suitable place to file his sermons and church records. There were two things available. One was the old iron safe. The other was a filing cabinet. The safe was an unhandy affair. The filing cabinet did not protect against fire. He wanted the good features of both. So he had a couple of local men build what he thought would fill the bill. He called it the Safe-Cabinet. When other people saw the Safe-Cabinet they wanted one, too. And so began a successful business in Marietta.

The question arises as to how to make knowledge come to the surface, as it were, when we need it. The best answer is that once we understand what our immediate problem is and what the process of creation is, we find our minds working in an easy manner and pulling out what we need when we want it.

Generally, when you deal with this sort of creation, you do not go outside the field of knowledge with which you are concerned. Usually you use the accumulated knowledge in a particular field. It is the real reason for accumulating such knowledge. The doctor uses it when he adapts a certain form of treatment to your case. Occasionally a doctor may vary the treatment, and then it is of sufficient importance to be written up in the medical journals. The research chemist uses it when he draws upon his knowledge of past chemical results. The mechanic draws upon his knowledge of putting a machine together.

You may think that you would like to invent a new cartoon feature. Incidentally, many owners of cartoon features *are* idea men; others do the actual drawing. "But what kind of feature?" you ask yourself. Now your adaptation is simple. You observe the Webster "Bridge" cartoons, representing a ridiculous feature of home life. You might think of another ridiculous feature of home life, such as television (Webster himself did), or proceed a step into business. Immediately a ridiculous feature of business comes to mind, the conference. Conferences are often to men what bridge is to women. A cartoon series could be made of "Crucial Conferences" with a little light on what goes on behind the doors. Or international conferences. Or congressional conferences. Or sales conventions. Or senate investigations. Maybe all of them, varied from day to day, depicting the life of the male. You see how your mind can gravitate from one idea to another, all closely related.

You observe the great success of self-help books. What kind of book should you write? It was said that the world was ready and waiting for books showing how to manage people. What else is the world waiting for? Go out and ask people. I once asked a university class of young people their greatest problem. What do you suppose they said? Almost every last one had an inferiority complex and wanted to know how to get rid of it.

Some of this working backwards is not as difficult as it sounds. No doubt you have already found yourself doing bits of it in connection with this book.

In advertising it is not so difficult to pick out a new attribute of a product and adapt it to an advertising campaign. A merchandising man simply looks over the obvious needs and desires of his prospective buyers and finds that his product meets those desires or remakes it so that it does.

Moving Backwards on Ideas

But other problems are more complex. You have to find something on which to begin. Many people had seen train wrecks, but, when George Westinghouse saw one, he decided to do something about it. He realized the need of more than hand-operated brakes. But what? He could not think of a solution. So he waited. One day he read of Italian engineers using compressed air for tunnel excavation. That then was something on which he could build in making his adaptation of airbrakes. So he devised an air compressing unit, which admitted or released pressure to the braking system.

Very often we have to search diligently to discover this thing upon which to build. The thing we know most about is the thing we propose to create. The more nebulous and hazy this is in our minds, the more difficult it is going to be to find it. Our first step is to see if we cannot better understand just what it is we seek.

Obviously, we must begin by examining this new thing of which we expect so much. Is it possible for us to narrow down its qualities? What do we want of it? What is it?

It is not just a new tree that we seek, perhaps, but a drouth-proof tree, one that will hold its own in long, dry years.

It is not just a rubber heel that we seek but one that does not wear off at the edges.

It is not just an ordinary air-conditioning plant but one that may be produced cheaply.

Here is a prescription for handling this particular type of creation:

1. Know what you are seeking. You cannot just be general and say, "I want more money," as one student suggested to me, and expect it to drop into your lap. But you can be specific, and say, "I am going to develop a new wear-forever rubber heel" or "devise a cheap system of air conditioning," and then proceed.

2. If it is not already obvious, you establish from your own analysis of your prospective creation its dominant attribute. In the case of the rubber heel, it is the quality of not wearing off at the end; in the case of air conditioning, it is a *cheap* home outfit.

3. What are the elements of this prospective attribute? Is there anything else that has this quality or attribute, preferably something that is related to yours? In the case of the rubber heels that won't wear off, there are all sorts of hard substances for the corner of the heel from metal that has already been used to other things. Maybe it would be harder, more lasting rubber in the part of the heel that usually wears off.

Could the problem of air conditioning be solved by quantity production? Which process lends itself most readily to cheap production? Or is there a new process, not patented? Maybe you should be going through the physics books for fundamental principles.

There are, in the case of trees, certain ones that naturally resist drouth. Could they be adapted to your country?

Backwards and Forward

It is rather obvious that once you have stepped back to find something on which to begin work, you will make many changes in moving forward again. And, of course, you may make several false starts, for what seems like a simple plan cannot always be adapted into the final result. That has happened many times in "cancer cures." The difficulty, of course, generally lies in not understanding fully the nature of the cancer problem and consequently the right thing to adapt.

You may make your own investigation; indeed, if your memory will not supply facts, you must go out and dig them up.

When newspapers began to appear, demand for paper skyrocketed. Enough rags from which paper was generally made could not be obtained. Who had a new source of material? The great discoverer was a hand weaver of linens, Gottlieb Keller. A friend who turned out handmade paper from rags had told him about the need.

He began making experiments, and he likewise began to keep his eyes open. A group of children, little appreciating that they were carrying out the initial steps in a great world experiment, were using a grindstone to cut holes in cherry pits which they turned into necklaces. The cherry pits were embedded in a piece of board for greater ease in holding them against the grindstone.

But Keller looked further than simply the making of children's necklaces. He was perhaps the first of those manufacturing geniuses who found a fortune in a by-product. For in a pool of water through which the grindstone was revolving, Keller saw a mass of pulverized wood and cherry stones. He reached down and picked up a handful, then squeezed out the water. To him it seemed much the same thing as the rag pulp that his friend was turning into paper.

He had found one of the world's great manufacturing processes—paper from wood pulp—and sold out to his friend, Heinrich Voelter, for $700. The great fortune was for others in later years.

Do you know how Kettering of General Motors got his "Duco"? He wanted a quick-drying paint or enamel. It was taking 17 days to paint the cheaper automobiles and 35 days for the more expensive ones. Kettering knew the outcome he wanted. But how was he to find the solution to the problem? You see, it was just the same sort of backward-solving problem that we are considering in this chapter.

His workmen told him that he could not solve the problem, that paint would not dry quickly enough to paint a car in an hour. Now Kettering began to observe. He wanted to find out if someone somewhere did not have a paint that had quick-drying properties. He was always looking for such paints. One day, walking down New York's Fifth Avenue, he saw some pin trays with a new type of lacquer on them. He called on the pin-tray manufacturer and found the origin of the paint.

It was made in a little laboratory back of a business block. "It would never do to finish automobiles," he was told. "It would dry before it hit the metal." Duco had its origin in what they had been using and what Kettering added. That was the way Kettering proceeded in his creation.

Charles Pfizer & Company wanted something more potent than penicillin, something that would kill more diseases. Five million dollars had already been spent on developments to make penicillin cheap enough so that everyone could enjoy its benefits, but the company was not satisfied. They wanted something beyond penicillin.

But what? Working backwards to find the unknown became a tremendous search extending to every corner of the world. The company screened 100,000 soil samples from everywhere. Seventy-five seemed to offer possibilities, but there were 75 failures among them. But then Number 76 came through, a powerful antibiotic weapon for the conquest of pneumonia, whooping cough, venereal infections, yaws, undulant fever, anthrax, typhus, and other dread diseases.

Terramycin had arrived.

Sometimes one works backwards and solves his problem. Then his idea is followed by hundreds of men making all sorts of adaptations simply by working forward. This happened in the case of color on machinery.

Its purpose is not, as many people suppose, simply to make machinery beautiful. A few decades ago a Massachusetts shoe manufacturer found one of his old workmen unable to keep up with production because of his eyes. The machinery was black; the leather with which the man worked was black. The manufacturer's thinking was not particularly difficult. His working backwards simply consisted in painting the machine in color. Other workmen in the factory followed the same plan and soon the plant was an array of colors. Later an adaptation was made—going forward— when the moving parts of the machinery were marked with contrasting colors. Soon other manufacturers followed the idea.

But then there was more moving backwards, as often happens. What colors were best? The light that bounces back from a surface is what counts. When a desk was painted light green or buff, it was just as good as installing another electric bulb. Floors, walls, and ceilings of factories then began to be brightened up. Later it was discovered that the best colors for huge machines were pale green, buff, and light gray.

Other studies—working backwards again while the big idea itself was going forward—were coming along. This time they were psychological ones. Light blue and yellow made coke ovens seem cooler to workers. Heavy objects could be made to seem light; square rooms could be made to appear rectangular and narrow rooms wide; ceilings could be lowered by color. Certain colors seemed to lend themselves even to certain types of thinking.

Color is also interesting to work with because it involves so many of the factors controlling our selection of attributes. The machinery problem was one involving labor-saving and the preservation and well-being of ourselves and others. But color more often today involves beauty and appeal to the senses and the fact of its being in the current of the world's thinking.

Remember the days when white, or lack of color, was emphasized in kitchens, bathrooms, and hospitals. Undoubtedly this was because white seemed to indicate cleanliness and freedom from germs and so seemed an aid to our well-being. But finally beauty and appeal to the senses became more powerful, and color was introduced in bathrooms and kitchens.

Today color is in the current of the world's thinking. This has become a color age. A generation ago we might have been horrified at the thought of a pink house, but today we accept it. However, it might be a battle to change the color of something long fixed by tradition. Fire trucks, for instance. Red belongs to fire although possibly yellow trucks would be as easily seen.

Color—what interesting possibilities for adaptation!

Some More Examples

You say to yourself: "I wish there were some way that we could have cheaper vegetables and fruits. I know I'd enjoy them myself, and I'm sure others would."

But how? Cheapness is what you want. You go down to your wholesale fruit dealer and you find the price thus and so. You figure spoilage, rent, and overhead, and you wonder how the little retail store can make a profit. So you go back and do some figuring. What are the factors that make the price so high? Original cost perhaps, but you often read that growers are willing to sell for almost nothing to get rid of the fruit or vegetables. Then the price you are asked must be consumed by transportation and middlemen's profits.

How do others handle such a situation? One idea is at hand, a motor truck of your own. I know a man who makes a good thing buying up a truckload of produce, bringing it home 600 miles, and selling it out. Probably you know others doing similar things.

Long before World War II, I was in the laboratory of one of the great wheat authorities of Russia. There in a room were over 30,000 different samples of wheat, both the grain and stalks, from all parts of the world. On the wall was a great map covered with criss-cross lines indicating the exact places in Russia and the corresponding places in other parts of the world where the same wheat was being grown or could be grown. What a foundation on which to work! It has not been generally known that for years Russia had agriculturists traveling throughout the world seeking new crop varieties that might be adapted to Russian conditions.

Nearly every country in the world is trying to find a better or more profitable use for its land. Southern Rhodesia is now producing five times as much flue-cured leaf tobacco as it did before World War II. It has not only learned that it can be done, but British buyers, restricted in dollar purchases in the United States, want it to do more. Even our North Carolina tobacco auctioneers over there in Southern Rhodesia are "singing mournful music for American growers of the leaf," as *The Wall Street Journal* expresses it.

Agriculturists use our backwards type of solution frequently. At an experimental farm of the United States Department of Agriculture, a new type of tomato was secured by this process of working backwards. It had been observed that tomatoes were being wiped out by rust. A new type was developed, but rust affected it also. Then, working backwards, someone remembered a funny little wild tomato that grew in Peru. Rust did not affect it, but it was not supposed to be edible. After numerous experiments in crossbreeding, the right kind of foolproof tomato was turned out.

Scientists create new animals today just as they create new plants, by the process of breeding. There are new cattle, new hogs, new poultry. One of the successful pioneers in this field is the great King Ranch in Texas. This is the ranch

[111]

where you drive for hours and hours, and you still find yourself on the same great property. It developed a cross between the shorthorn found on so many farms of the Middle West and the Braham cattle of India which, through long generations, had learned not to mind the heat.

The Beltsville farm of the United States Department of Agriculture has been breeding a hog, through some 17 years, that has a high percentage of meat and a low percentage of lard. Small turkeys have been developed for small families as well as chickens with larger breasts and drumsticks.

The basic principle here is simple. The point is to find intial stock that has the right characteristics and then cross it with stock that has other wanted characteristics. For instance, efforts are now successful in crossing the ordinary Jersey cow with a cow from India in order to produce a dairy cow that will stand our southern heat and yet produce plenty of milk.

How many possibilities there are for all of us in our spare time! Creating things is far more interesting and valuable than playing cards or working at crossword puzzles. For the most part, one's own creations will deal with one's own business or occupation because the earning of a reasonable living seems a paramount problem. What methods can you adapt to your own affairs to create a new future for you? What are the most pressing needs of your employer? Can you find a way to supply those needs? Work backwards and see what you can do about them, as we have done in this chapter. There is a great field of activity here, covering everything from business to science, art to music, school teaching to professional writing.

{9

Every Man Can Be a Creative Scientist

Aʟᴇxᴀɴᴅᴇʀ Gʀᴀʜᴀᴍ Bᴇʟʟ one day paid a visit to Joseph Henry, secretary of the Smithsonian Institution. He had come on another matter but casually mentioned the idea of talking over a wire, a thought with which he had been playing and experimenting. He explained to Henry what the idea really seemed to be and wondered whether, like a scientist, he should write a paper on the subject and let others do what they could with it or attempt to do the job himself.

"You have the germ of a great invention," encouraged Henry. "Work at it."

"But I don't have enough electrical knowledge to do it," replied Bell.

"Get it!" admonished Henry.

So Bell got the technical knowledge, and we got the telephone.

Scientific achievement is now much more complex and difficult than in the days of Bell and Henry. But—and remember this—there is also much more to work with. While civilization presents more obstacles, there are more ways to get around obstacles than ever before. And because there are more things to work with, there are more opportunities for profitable endeavor. Every industry seems to have its hundred sidelines. Each may be an opportunity in itself.

Industry and government spend billions of dollars a year in research and experimentation. Finding things out and making use of the findings have become big business.

Most people, though, look at a scientist with awe. He is supposed to be an unapproachable individual in a long white coat. Behind the locked doors of his laboratory he stands surrounded by evil-smelling test tubes. Every now and then he is expected to emulate the magician and pull a rabbit out of the test tube in the shape of a cure for cancer or old age.

But it isn't like that at all. Being a scientist is more a state of mind. The great scientist may not deal with test tubes nearly as much as he does with facts and ideas. The man whom one sees in the laboratory today may be doing only routine work while the big idea and the problems involved are being thought out by the man at the mahogany desk upstairs.

The strange and unhappy fact is that many men in science are not idea men at all. And there hangs quite a story, for one of the great problems in industry today is how to cause men who are supposedly idea men to have more ideas. Here is part of a letter from one of the great corporations:

"We have over 1,000 graduate engineers here. One of the ways in which these engineers can be of most use to us is by using their imaginations and by doing creative thinking. Consequently we feel that we have a real problem. We are particularly interested in what type of text or material you use and how the class meetings themselves are conducted. We have been doing some work on this problem ourselves and so far have met with practically little success."

And Professor John E. Arnold of the Massachusetts Institute of Technology writes me: "For a number of years now the mechanical engineering department of M.I.T. has been giving serious thought to the problem of developing more creative engineers. We are concerned over the tremendous mass of factual data that must be absorbed by our students in four short years and feel that it may have a stifling effect on their imagination and creative ability.

"To counteract this trend, we have started a course in product design. This course is devoted entirely to studying the creative process and other non-analytical problems of design. It has been well received by students, staff and administrators and the program is growing rapidly. It has recently been formalized as the creative engineering laboratory."

We can be sure that creation is a pressing need even in the great corporation.

It was Christian Steenstrup, holder of 126 patents and close associate of Steinmetz and Edison, who put his finger on the problem. "For the reason that originality is not related to education, you may find good ideas coming from all levels of workers," he said. J. F. Lincoln, president of Lincoln Electric of Cleveland, declared that one of the troubles today is the lack of recognition that people who work with their hands also have the ability to think. Douglas Lurton, who created *Your Life* magazine as his idea, feels that a man with an eighth-grade education who develops his creative power has a better chance at a successful life than a Harvard graduate who does not understand the possibilities of creation.

But readers of this book have earlier perceived the point that creative thinking is something quite different from ordinary educational mind stuffing. Comparatively few educational institutions emphasize creation.

There is a great deal of misunderstanding about this matter of scientific thinking and its relation to the matter of producing original ideas. Let us, as the orator suggested, see if we can "unscrew the inscrutable."

Thousands of people who would be mightily surprised if anyone told them they were scientists actually have scientific minds, and thousands of others who like to call themselves scientists are not scientific at all. In spite of all their playing with test tubes and microscopes, the latter have never really discovered or created anything. They are simply duplicating the work of others or carrying out the instructions of someone else "to see if it works."

A scientist discovers some fact or relationship that has not been generally apparent up to that time. He may let it go at that, or he may go ahead and build upon what he has found and produce an entirely new creation, as Alexander Graham Bell did. But all the time he is working he keeps his eyes open to see if perchance something else valuable might also turn up along the way.

The scientist is often called a child at heart because to him everything is one big question mark. "The investigator is one in whom this natural curiosity still persists," Walter B. Cannon told the graduating class at Yale Medical School many years ago. "He has never got past the annoying stage of asking 'Why?' The events occurring on every side which are matters of course to most men, startle him into wonderment."

The reason for scientific education is to enable a young man to learn how to use the tools of the profession and to attain a background of what has been done before in order that he may build upon it. It should give a man a tremendous assortment of ideas on which he may create new things later on. Many times, of course, it does not. In my own student days at Columbia University I found the most valuable courses to be those that had the power of presenting a great number of idea-producing thoughts.

Research is deliberate observation—hunting up something to observe—while ordinary observation is simply seeing what goes on before one. But the latter is sometimes more valuable than the former.

Life of a Scientist

The secret life of a scientist is something like this:

First, he gathers facts, and more facts, and still more facts about his proposed undertaking, just as Bell did for his telephone. He wants to know, if possible, everything that everyone else has learned about it before.

Second, at the same time he is gathering facts, he is observing and observing and observing. The germ of the very thing he seeks may be on the next street corner or in a little store or shop. Kettering kept his eyes open in such places. Remember where he found the inspiration for his lacquer.

Third, all the time he is gathering facts and watching for things, his mind is also unconsciously working over the vast amount of knowledge he has assembled in his lifetime. It may someday—or more often in the middle of the night—hand him an interesting tidbit that he has all but forgotten.

Fourth, when he has a few ideas from his process of working backwards, he begins his forward experiments. Will the procedure he has thought out really work?

Fifth, and we mustn't forget this, all the while he is experimenting, he keeps observing what is before him. He is looking into the interesting sidelines.

The Wall Street Journal announced one day that the colonels, majors, and captains in the Pentagon were using a "new" word—"serendipity." Horace Walpole created the word around 1754 after he had read a nice fairy story called "The Three Princes of Serendip." And what were the three princes of Serendip doing? Well, they remind one of modern businessmen gathering up ideas here, there, and everywhere. "As their highnesses traveled they were always making discoveries, by accident or sagacity, of things they were not in quest of," wrote Walpole.

Every schoolboy knows that Columbus discovered the Western Hemisphere while looking for a shorter route to the Indies. And it was an accident that led Pasteur to a ready means of creating immunity to many diseases by inoculation. He had been working in his laboratory producing cholera in chickens by injecting cultures of fowl cholera bacillus. One day, when he came back to work after vacation, he used some cultures that had been lying there in the laboratory all summer. But the chickens did not die.

From a new cholera outbreak, he secured some fresh cultures. With them, he inoculated some chickens that he had just bought at the market and included among them the fowls that had resisted the previous inoculation. But, strangely enough, the new chickens all died while the ones that had the previous inoculation lived.

Here, apparently, was a ready means of creating immunity to infectious diseases, a goal toward which other scientists had also been making progress. The observation was this: a weak culture of the bacillus, when used for inoculation, created immunity, so why not use weak cultures deliberately? This would prevent chickens from catching the disease. By following the same principles of adaptation we have mentioned earlier in this book, Pasteur and other scientists could substitute other diseases for fowl cholera and other animals, and even humans, for chickens.

Alexander Fleming, an English bacteriologist, noticed that pus-producing bacteria were dissolved by a mould that contaminated them. That was the beginning of penicillin. A Danish investigator, Dam, and his associates noticed that animals on restricted diets often suffered hemorrhages. He discovered it to be due to the lack of a substance, now known as Vitamin K and found in many cereals. All of these were side issues of the original work, but they were of world importance.

Now comes the time for more ideas and maybe more experiments in the great task of proving and promoting the venture. The scientist may have to do this by himself or the corporation's sales department may take it in hand. When Kettering had a quick-drying enamel lacquer ready for cars, he found opposition in the company. So one day he invited his opponent to lunch. Kettering arranged that the luncheon should drag on a bit. When they came out of the building, there was his opponent's car all newly finished and ready for use. Kettering won the battle for the quick-drying finish right there.

What a time they had in finding a way to administer chaulmoogra oil, which has proved of such great benefit in treating leprosy. Some of the lepers said that they would just as soon have leprosy as to take chaulmoogra oil, which made them deathly sick. But, when given hypodermically, the oil was not absorbed properly.

The doctors asked Merck & Company what to do. It was out of their immediate experience, Merck & Company said, but from unverified knowledge they judged that adding camphor to the prescription would make it absorb. So it proved.

But is the scientist done? No, indeed!

He has to work out a whole list of by-products from the experiment, particularly if he has not already picked some up along the way, until, in the language of the packing house, there is nothing left but the squeal. For often, by-products mean the difference between profit and loss in a business.

And strange by-products there are. Who would think, for example, of a fire extinguisher having any relation to licorice candy? But it does have. Foamite Firefoam is a product that originated with MacAndrews & Forbes, the great dealers in and processors of licorice root. Every schoolboy knows the principle that a fire cannot burn when oxygen is cut off. The licorice people saw, in processing the root, that after they had drawn off the licorice extract and added soda ash to what remained they had a liquid of extraordinary foaming power. It billowed up, covered everything, and stuck to everything. So when it is projected on a stubborn fire, it just cuts off all the oxygen and the fire is out.

Is the scientist through yet? No, because by the time he has done all this, some competitor will have something "just as good," and he will have to devise a still better product or something entirely new to keep the factory busy.

Procter & Gamble are trying to find out, among other things, how to reduce the amount of bacteria left on an average person's hands after washing (what an advertising idea that would be!), what happens to the human skin on prolonged exposure to soap, and how to preserve the natural Vitamin E that helps prevent rancidity in vegetable shortenings.

Arthur L. Stahl, University of Miami professor, was a pioneer in developing frozen concentrated orange juice. But was his job ended? No, indeed. If he could do so much for surplus oranges, why not take a look at little known tropical plants and see if they could not be given a commercial boost as well? So he has such interesting things as guava, papaya, mango, and Barbados cherry with which to work. There are many tropical fruits that contain much more Vitamin C than orange juice. He envisions the time when the processed fruit industry of southern Florida will be far greater than it is and his own work at the university will be self-supporting from royalties derived from new products.

The frozen food people have been hunting for more and

more products to take the place of those crowding the market. There are even such varied things as chop suey, waffles, and pizza. One woman varied the attribute of common frozen lemonade and turned out frozen pink lemonade with such success that she could have sold three times the amount if she had had it. She may have difficulty when others go into colored lemonade and prepare it for the freezer cabinet. But perhaps she will then have a new variation. A Colorado woman made a great success in selling frozen cooky dough.

Finding Things out for Yourself

Newton may have discovered the law of gravity, but there are plenty of minor laws yet to be discovered all about us, laws that do not require great laboratories and a corps of scientists. They do require us to use our heads, however.

The nature of great original thinking is not so different whether it be in science or business. I have purposely mixed such examples to show the likeness. This thought may sound like heresy to some of the scientific brethren in the colleges, but it needn't. For creation has its own principles.

After all, the procedure of the scientist is not greatly different from that of a man producing successful ideas in any field of endeavor, whether it be business, finance, or government. He has to gather facts and things and build upon them.

"Research is a high-hat word that scares a lot of people," remarked Kettering. "It needn't. It is rather simple. Essentially it is nothing but a state of mind, a friendly welcoming toward change. The research state of mind can apply to anything—personal affairs or any kind of business, big or little."

I think it would have been a lot of fun to have seen Kettering batting his way through General Motors, don't you? Kettering had reality, originality, and practicality. To achieve acceptance of ideas, one often has to have that combination of thinking.

A great deal of the difficulty in working with an idea arises because of our inability to get at the facts in previous procedures of the kind. "What's been going on here?" we sometimes ask ourselves when we learn the facts.

For instance, you hear much about the money being made in real estate. You hear of "old families owning half the town." So you buy a house or maybe an apartment house and soon find that you cannot sell it for what you have in it. You hear of great fortunes that have been made all about you, but likewise all about are people who have lost money even in an inflationary period.

So you begin to investigate. Is there somewhere a principle that seems to hold good and work in real estate investment as it does in scientific fields? You begin to look here, there, and everywhere. You talk with dozens of people.

Finally, you find Jim. Jim is a character with his diploma *cum laude* from the famous College of Experience. But he would not like to have his real name mentioned here since then people would automatically raise the price when they found that Jim was the prospective buyer. "It must be worth more, or Jim wouldn't be thinking of it," they would say.

Here is one of Jim's modest adventures. What he bought was against the judgment of many people. Indeed the real estate company was having a hard time selling it. It consisted of a row of rather dilapidated flats on the main cross street just a couple of blocks from the hotel. The price was a modest one, $25,000. It had been marked down from $30,000. But the man most interested in that locality wouldn't give more than $20,000. Jim bought it at $25,000 and paid $8,000 down.

He began to experience the vicissitudes of a landlord. Just about every penny that he got out of it the first two years seemed to go right back in. When the steps didn't fall down, the plaster did; and when the plumbing was fixed, the heating plant would fizzle.

You may think this is going to be a story of how not to do it. But no! Jim has his realty formula down pat and more valuable to him than Newton's law of gravity. After four years, he was offered $40,000 for the old flats people thought no good. Deducting the $10,000 remaining on the mortgage, he found that he had made $8,000 grow to $30,000 in four years.

What had been going on during those years? Down the street, a block away, a four-story building was going up. Three blocks away, a great new department store was blocking the horizon. The cross street was eclipsing the main street of the city.

Now Jim did not know absolutely that such things were going to happen soon, nor did anyone else. But Jim knew that they would happen sooner or later and that all he had to do was wait, providing his modest investment would work off the mortgage with something extra for winter and summer vacations.

Jim discovered and demonstrated a basic real estate principle that struck me as quite important. "Look here," said

Jim, talking out of the textbook of the College of Experience, "don't do like so many people. Never buy a fancy building at a good price in a receding location. If you do, you'll lose your shirt. You've got too much money tied up in the building, which can never increase in value because the location is going the other way. An ideal setup is the old building with a good location, a place that nobody wants and is going cheap because it looks so dreadful. You don't have to think about inflation or deflation if the location is improving or bound to improve. Most of your money is in the land and, if the building deteriorates, you should worry."

There were some other interesting points in this true story. The government was allowing Jim a nice $900 a year nontaxable depreciation on the old building because it hardly seemed that it could last more than twelve or fifteen years. Depreciation—that was a nice thing. "Most people don't think about that," Jim explained. "And, if I sell out, I pay only about half as much income tax as the fellow who works and earns that money. It's capital gains, you see. My real estate operations? They are just bright ideas, that's all."

One afternoon I was lounging by the swimming pool at one of the great desert hotels at Tucson, Arizona. Fresh from a dip in the Pacific Ocean that morning, there had arrived by air a man all set to get a desert tan and swim that afternoon in Tucson. Quite casually, I asked him whether or not he thought the contractors building houses all over the country were really making any money.

He looked at me like a long lost brother. "I wanted the answer to that question myself. No one would tell me," he replied. "So I built 50 of the houses as an experiment to find out. I made $50,000 doing it, and so I can answer that generally they have made money." In fact, he was so enthusiastic over what he had demonstrated to himself in California that he was out looking for more places to build more houses.

The crux of such building projects was this, he found out—to pick only localities where the demand was insistent. "I ran across one builder who can't even sell two-bathroom houses with landscaped yards for $8500. He's in a town where there's too much building," he explained.

There was no deep research to his fact finding, but all around you are fundamental questions that stump a person when he tries to get the answer. What really goes on in a successful undertaking that differentiates it from the many unsuccessful ones? Often those engaged in the business are not too anxious to give away what they regard as their trade secrets. Sometimes, to tell the truth, they actually have difficulty in putting their finger on the secrets of their own success.

The opportunities for research and investigation even in small things are enormous. Any man who can't save a few hundred or a few thousand by finding a better way to accomplish something in everyday life is not using his head. I know many people who enjoy a good deal of luxury without too much expense because they hunt out unusual ideas. Take this matter of travel, for instance. Nothing irks me more than to see people taking what they get out of the ticket window without the slightest thought and then finding that they have everything wrong but the destination.

For example, as a cornfed Middle Westerner who knows the value of a dollar, I discovered a while back that it was almost as cheap to buy a first-class rail ticket from a Nebraska point to Jacksonville, Florida, and return, than to buy one to Washington, D. C., and yet one could go to Jacksonville by way of Washington. How much nicer, too, when you have to go to Washington! You also go down to the Carolinas for a bit, try Florida and the Gulf Coast, spend a few days in New Orleans and Houston, and finally home, with the fare about the same as it would have been had they shot you through to Washington and back on an overcrowded train.

Now, as one thinks this over, what a wonderful promotional idea for all those Florida and Gulf Coast and Texas people. See it all on one ticket! Get everybody heading back east to take a look at something down south, too. But I don't think those boosters have caught on as yet.

And what wonderful opportunities for around the world travel via far-off Australia and New Zealand. One may travel by air to the Southern Hemisphere, choose a luxurious boat to England via India and the Mediterranean, and come back from England first class for less than $1,500. Yet many travel agents want to ship you straight through by the traditional around-the-world route and charge you $500 more. The reason, of course, is that the big English boats between Australia and England figure their rates on the low English pound. When I asked a travel agent about such trips, he looked at me in blank amazement. He had not the slightest idea how such things were done. In fact, he did not think they were done at all. It remained for a Los Angeles travel man to dig it all up and feature the plan. What an idea this is for all those people in the Southern Hemisphere who are seeking American dollars!

Big or Little Things?

It is not so difficult to find things that you would like to see invented or accomplished. But working backwards over a project is, of course, much harder than working forward where you simply run across an immediate adaptation. It is wonderful mental exercise, however, to turn over possibilities that require research and working backwards.

For the fun of it, sit down some evening and create your own vision of the future. Start right in your own home. Start with one thing, and then ask what else. Let your mind wander from one idea to another.

Appliance manufacturers just love to think up new things for the home, but what do you dream up sitting there in your easy chair? Let the mind travel.

Now that we have air conditioning, what else? A new system or an addition to what we now have? Perfumed air? Maybe, maybe not. But possibly something that will give the conditioned air that perpetual soft touch that one experiences on a perfect spring day. Maybe people would like that. Perhaps the chorophyll or deodorant boys should get busy and do something for those systems that seem to pump up stale basement air hour after hour. Are all the germs filtered out of conditioned air or not? I don't know; I suspect not. Should air be treated with ultra violet rays or not? What an advertising argument for theaters, railway cars, hospitals, and schools that their air is germ free.

That is what I mean. Just let your mind wander around a bit.

The family washing machine has now grown into an

almost automatic device for washing and drying clothes. How will we attain easier dry cleaning? And what about easier ironing? Or, are textiles all going to be made so that they will need no ironing? And are they to be spotproof to eliminate most dry cleaning? Are commercial laundries and dry cleaning establishments going to find other services to perform?

What shall we do for television? Color is coming. Cheap sets are here, unless we aspire to become the Henry Ford of television and turn out a regular set for next to nothing. Maybe we could think up some new uses for television. I once ran across a school in Galveston where the principal, through a communicating system, could listen in on any schoolroom at any time. He pushed a button and in came the English recitation from Room 9 or arithmetic from Room 17. Intercommunicating television might be an improvement on that. As a matter of fact, one prison uses TV to check on both prisoners and guards. Maybe we could have a system whereby a woman could see what was going on in the sick room and who was at the door, or telephones where the talkers would see each other—that is, if they were presentable and wanted to be seen.

Now we come to the crux of the matter. You say to me: "Some of these things are too complicated and would require too much capital. I'm not Alexander Graham Bell." What we have dreamed about in the preceding paragraphs gave us quite an assortment of things that could be done. The natural answer to your observation is that we do not make use of all the ideas and possibilities for working backwards that occur to us. We pick and choose. Some of the aids to air conditioning are probably not too difficult for a man with a leaning toward chemistry, drugs, and medicine. The television suggestions, while tough on the uninitiated, might be dead simple for the electrical manufacturer. Every man may well dream in his own field. For the ordinary man, the sidelines may be more profitable than the main line.

Take the case of the automobile. Gone are the old days when half a dozen mechanics could work in a back shop and turn out cars in a profitable way. Even then, the automobile industry was crowded with failures. There were narrow escapes. Years ago a banking family in our old home town had to meet the payroll of the Buick company one week. But that, fortunately, became their profitable entree into General Motors later on.

You might today have a wonderful idea for a new type of automobile, perhaps an atomic-powered automobile. But developing the principles of such a thing would be a tremendous undertaking. And you add to it the task of financing and selling the automobile. The cost does not permit ordinary people to play around with a new automobile name when it takes several million dollars to get a model in production. Plenty of good names have disappeared in our lifetime. Remember Marmon, Jordan, Stutz—all splendid cars in their class.

But what does this suggest? If we are automobile-minded does it mean that we are to stop dead in our tracks? It suggests rather that all the sidelines incident to the automobile business are the ones for the small man. Every great industry creates thousands of side opportunities. The other day I met a wealthy man. Finally I happened to ask him what he did. "Oh," he laughed, "I just melt up a few old car batteries." Thousands of stores and shops have for their sole business the sale of renewal parts, both new and second-hand, for low-priced cars. Others exist because they wash your car in a few minutes.

In the idea business you have to be practical-minded. You can go just as far as you like. You may turn out to be another Bell or Kettering. Or you may only be the fellow who sells a few million trifles through the dime store. But either way you use your head.

Finally, do not get the idea that everything you see is scientifically conceived and tested. Many things that appear very, very scientific were very, very simple, while other things that appear simple made a lot of trouble.

I suppose you think that the Chevrolet people spent a lot of time and effort working out their trademark. You can picture all the bright minds of the organization taking home their brief cases and laboriously working into the wee hours of the morning drawing circles, triangles, and oblongs. You can picture the psychologists being called in to weigh the drawing power of these efforts.

The fact is that they did put in quite a bit of work on the matter, but it all wound up by W. C. Durant's looking at a piece of wallpaper. He liked the pattern and adapted the central design for the trademark.

You, too, can be a scientist, for science is only gathering the right fundamentals and then doing something about them. The beginnings of ideas are everywhere waiting for the eager eye and mind to seize.

How to Solve Problems Creatively

IT WAS A COLD, half-freezing day in a Nebraska spring, just the kind of day not to be down and out in Omaha.

The great depression was over the land, and the man I am writing about did not have money for a meal. There was only a quarter in his pocket.

What should he do? Most of us might have thought we were ready for the Salvation Army or the City Mission or even the Missouri River.

Should he spend the quarter for a sandwich and a cup of coffee, or should he be bolder and start right off in business?

For most men it would not have been the kind of day on which to start anything. Few stores expected to do much, and their expectations were being realized.

Looking at the dismal day before him, our man had an

idea. By George, it was just the right sort of day for an idea of that kind, too. A day when automobile windshields were quite undecided whether to freeze or fog was just the opportunity for him. He had been an observing man, and he had noted one time a peculiar German soap that seemed to prevent windshields from freezing up in bad weather. He hunted up a drug store and invested his quarter in a cake of that soap.

Then he began making the rounds of the filling stations. He would demonstrate the remarkable qualities of this "new" weather repellent, and he would end up by shaving off a little piece of the soap and selling it to the station man or his customer for a quarter. Sometimes he would get a double fifty-cent order. Then, having recovered his original capital and something for coffee and a sandwich, he hurried back to the drug store and bought another cake.

And still another! And another after that! By the end of the day he found that he was not only not going to have to sleep in the gutter but he also had a business.

I am not going to tell you the name of the man. To him, the memory must always be a painful one. But today he has a prosperous chemical company in Michigan.

What do you think of this fellow? I think we might as well give him a diploma as a creative problem solver, and if, by chance, he is reading this chapter, he may simply skip it and go on to the next. He doesn't need it.

Our time might properly be known as the age of problems. There are thousands of problems all about us. The entire world is a problem. Governments are full of problems, homes are full of problems, individuals have a daily diet of them. The Lincoln, Nebraska, high school has a class where the students solve problems of their own—not the mathematical kind—but personal and school troubles.

Problems are something like the measles: they spread from one person to another; they jump the boundaries of nations. Everything and everyone is in a dither. Nor does one expect the situation to improve, for this is a world of change, and the more change the more problems. Each solution of a problem brings more problems.

There is a story about a boy taking long strides along the avenue in company with his economy-minded father. "Why do you take such long steps, son?"

"To save shoe leather, papa."

"Wonderful, Johnny!" said the father; then he thought a moment and added, "Be careful you don't split your pants."

Creative problem solving is usually working backwards, a matter to which we have already paid attention. But now that we have looked into the scientist's approach to creation, we may find it easier to deal further with that intricate and important matter of working backwards and of solving problems creatively.

A problem is probably differentiated to most minds from ordinary creative desire by the urgency with which it confronts one. It comes smack against one. In ordinary creation, whether we are working forward or backwards, we are not so pressed for a decision. Anything that we create is an extra dividend out of life. But when a problem strikes us, we have to do something or suffer loss in one way or another.

The very fact that there is a problem means that an alternative is confronting us, but it is such an undesirable solution that we do not want to take it. Our Omaha friend might have slept on a park bench, for that was the unhappy solution the problem offered of itself. The problem says to us: "Find a better way or do what I tell you." And we have to beat the problem with a better alternative. A big smashing answer to the problem may lay it out completely.

The difference between a great man and an ordinary man is often his ability to solve problems creatively. Many people think that anyone who solves a problem is creative-minded. Nothing is further from the truth. He is just a "routiner" unless he can produce a new solution to a problem of consequence.

Most of our entire upbringing and education, in home and school, deal with the routine solution of problems. There is the problem of cold weather, and we are introduced to the clothes we should wear. There is the problem of eating, and we are introduced to the food we should eat and the forks and knives that go with it. We are taught to write in the customary way in order that we may communicate with other people. We learn how to put our letters in the post office and our money in the bank. But this is all rather commonplace. This is largely plain imitation, doing what the other fellow does.

And there are some people who like to make problems out of nothing. It does not matter much whether we go to the movies Monday or Tuesday, whether we wear the brown or the gray suit, whether we have beef stew or stewed beef. It is not too much of a task to decide whether to spend 32 cents for a tube of tooth paste at one store or walk three blocks farther and get it for 29 cents. It really does not make much difference. Of course, occasionally, there are special consequences, but not very often.

The story used to be told in educational circles of the

California college president who answered most of his mail and solved the routine problems contained therein by the simple process of letting it accumulate. After a month or so, he found that the little problems had generally solved themselves anyway.

There are many books that deal with problems, but the only problems worth worrying about are those that involve obvious consequences. And those are the ones worth a creative solution. Such a problem involves considerable time, money, or possibly an entire future. There are people who go through life solving all sorts of petty routine problems but never a consequential one.

Again, a creative solution brings the hearer or reader up with a start. It makes him exclaim "Gee whiz!" And he adds, "I'd never have thought of doing it that way."

The man who solves his problems by rule of thumb may find his solution completely outmoded by the man with a creative idea. For example, the ordinary real estate man just tacks up a sign, "For Sale." But not William Zeckendorf in New York. He saw in the old riding stable he had purchased near Central Park not just a livery barn or a building to be torn down but a wonderful place for a television studio. So, instead of a loss, he had a profit of $600,000 by selling it to ABC for television. In fact, his specialty is making money by finding new uses for property.

To most people the bluffs back of the main part of El Paso were just useless hills worth $100 an acre. But a few enterprising men decided to do something; they built houses in those locations, and almost before one could sense what was going on, there was a newly fashionable part of the city.

It is of course obvious that before one attacks any problem

he must understand what the problem is. In that respect problem solving is a bit different from ordinary working backwards where you already have an idea of what you would like to accomplish. The problem just flies in at the window unannounced.

Richard Trevithick had built a locomotive, but it broke too many rails. The trouble and resulting problem, however, were with the rails and not the engine. In 1811, Blenkinsop thought he saw a difficulty in rail transportation—that of securing traction. He "solved it" by producing a rack and pinion railroad. But that was wholly unnecessary in ordinary country. There wasn't any problem.

We hear much of that vague term called human relations. So let us take a look at a human relations problem right from the capital city of Texas, a problem where finding out what it was all about virtually solved the problem itself.

The telephone bell was ringing in the best telephone fashion—loud and clangy and imperious—demanding attention before breakfast. One might have known that trouble was in the making somewhere. And Our Good Woman was not to be disappointed. What the telephone was trying to say in jagged squawks was always best related later on by the husband's unabridged translation "that hell had broken loose in the Home for Girls," of which Our Good Woman was one of the most valued trustees. The telephone conveyed the cheerful news that the girls were tearing about in great style, that they had been deprived of breakfast as a disciplinary measure, and the further flash news that they had at that moment locked the matron up.

Soon Our Good Woman was on the way to the home, excited by the prospect of adventure. When she arrived at the home, the battle tide had turned slightly. The matron had been succored from her peculiar situation in the closet and was now standing there awaiting reinforcements in the shape of Our Good Woman.

"Don't go in that room!" the matron exclaimed, throwing up her arms in a warning gesture. *"The girls are in there."*

Our Good Woman calmly swung open the door and entered.

There really were just two ordinary solutions most people would have thought of: crack down on the girls by main strength and subdue the rioters; or preach to them and lay down the law—tell 'em "what's what."

But Our Good Woman had a different solution. Before the girls could make up their minds whether or not they would like it, she was hurrying them over to her own home. Annie, the maid, got breakfast, all the time twisting her eyes around to see what strange new idea had come into Our Good Woman's head. Our Good Woman helped, and the girls helped and, almost before you knew it, there was breakfast and everybody eating.

After breakfast, Our Good Woman set out to find the real state of affairs, what the problem really was. Like so many, many situations in this world, the whole thing had been unintentional. Funny thing, too, that someone had been trying to do good in the world and had caused the trouble. A women's organization had decided that it would be a nice thing to do something pleasant for the girls in the home. But the woman who came to do the inviting to the party made the great mistake that so many people make in dealing with others.

The young girls accepted the invitation with alacrity, they

were all for going. But the older girls held back and declined the invitation, because, when it was offered, the woman doing the inviting somehow conveyed to the girls' minds the impression that they were regarded as charity girls. And could anything be more bitter? It just hurt too much, and they didn't feel like going and being publicly hurt some more. They told the matron they wouldn't go, and the matron said that was not being courteous and polite, and they would have to do without their breakfasts in consequence. That was the last straw for the girls. They were to be compelled to be hurt.

It just seemed that everybody was being impolite. Our Good Woman told the girls that they would not have to go to the party, soothed their wounded feelings, and treated them as equals. The girls then decided that they would go, after all. And that was that. Everything was calm and peaceful. And all were sorry that they had been so ununderstanding.

But in less skillful hands than those of Our Good Woman, what might not have happened? How many strikes, riots, and even battles have taken place because someone did not understand! In solving problems, facts have to come before action.

Those Tricky Financial Problems

Most problems that one encounters seem to be financial ones. In fact, that word "problem" always seems to imply figures. Making money—and losing it too—can be terribly important. If you doubt the interest in the subject, notice the number of financial and business advisory services. But how tragic it is when they have the wrong solution to problems and the advice turns out to be bad.

When financial trouble threatens someone in the family, it is time to call a conference of all members of the family. A famous columnist told me that he did so. All the other members of the family chipped in and financed a roadside market for the unfortunate one and, "Now," said the columnist, "he's making more than any of the rest of us."

Any man or company that makes or sells things is always confronted by at least four basic problems. Anything that answers any of these four questions is a contender as a successful idea:

1. How can we turn out our products more cheaply?

2. How can we get more money for them?

3. How can we broaden the uses of our products and increase their number?

4. How can we keep our business moving up and not down?

In fact, the solution of all four problems would be the average company's ideal. Remington Rand, for example, urges its employees to furnish ideas that increase sales, cut expenses, improve products, and create new outlets. All of these have for their final aim the making of profits.

And, as we have indicated before, the unusual solution to a problem may be the most valuable. One of the great railroads consulted a high-priced public relations firm as to what could be done to secure some passengers on what it believed was its best train. The advice was not to spend money on advertising but to serve a sumptuous dinner for the money. That was done, and business soon picked up.

During the dismal thirties, the Wayne Knitting Mills

found itself with a problem. It was the great problem everywhere those years—how to make ends meet. Plenty of companies could make hosiery. Cutting prices indefinitely meant loss. Who had a bright and daring idea? It would have to be one that would make women want to buy hosiery made by the Wayne Knitting Mills rather than by some other company.

In those days stockings were stockings, all being made in 30- and 31-inch lengths and all in the same size leg, varying only in the foot size. Over at the Vassar Company, an affiliate of Wayne, something else was observed—that women did not all have the same size and shape of leg. Why should there not be hosiery to fit all types?

A Boston company had tried stockings in different lengths, but Wayne Knitting Mills decided to go the whole way, abandon the production of average-length stockings, and turn out hosiery not only in different lengths but in four different leg sizes. They were to be known as Belle-Sharmeer hosiery. In a few brief years the idea proved itself, and Wayne Knitting was becoming a very profitable hosiery company. The idea had solved the problem and saved the day.

Let us turn for a moment to investment problem solving, a field in which ideas are valuable indeed. An elderly lady, whom I know well, has large quantities of government "E" bonds. You know, those are the popular government bonds that you bought during and after the war. They were issued originally for ten-year periods. When they become payable you may keep them for approximately another ten years. But until you turn them in, you do not receive any interest.

But our lady wants current interest, year by year, on her

bonds. All right, the government says, as these bonds mature, from year to year, turn them in and buy another series that pays yearly interest. But, the minute you turn them in, you have to pay income tax on the whole period you have owned them, roughly your usual rate of income tax on the $25 interest included in each $100 you get back. In other words, the government asks you to settle up right away on that "interest profit" you have made.

Our lady is a smart lady, and she is not satisfied with that arrangement, as explained by the bank. She wants current interest without at the present time having to make up that back tax.

How can she do it?

Fortunately I was working on that very problem for a financial weekly a few months before and had it at hand. It required simply a little observation and then working backwards. You turn those bonds over and read that fine print. Each bond has a specific value that increases year by year. You see, there is a reason for not wanting to cash those bonds ahead of time because, in later years, that interest is accumulating at a rate of better than 4 per cent to make up for that low interest the bonds were accumulating in earlier years.

The problem now is: you would like to have that interest to spend every year, but you don't want to pay the accumulated tax. Your thought leads you to something similar to a trust fund. After all, what concerns you is not individual bonds but the whole accumulation of bonds. When you draw money from a trust fund, you do not think of individual securities but income from the whole fund. So what could be simpler than just adding up the accumulating interest for the year and then turning in a few matured bonds for that amount? Then let the rest of the bonds go on accumulating interest.

Suppose the accumulated interest for one year is $300. From the government's point of view you are just cashing three $100 bonds. The interest on these amounts to $75 and so the tax in most cases would probably be negligible. But from your point of view you are getting a $300 return from the investment, largely tax free.

But suppose you had done what so many people are doing and followed the usual solution. Suppose you had $10,000 worth of bonds maturing and you changed to an interest-paying bond. The first thing you would have done would have been to settle up the tax on $2,500 interest. That would have cut down the principal amount you would have available for the new bonds. Then, each year, you would be paying a tax on the current interest you received. Suppose it were $300. Your interest this way is all taxable whereas only one-fourth as much or $75 dollars is taxable under our plan.

Of course you may say, "Well, I have to pay the tax sometime." Our answer is that income taxes may be lower one of these days. Then, too, you may have a bad year financially sometime and you can turn in the entire amount and permit your losses to offset your profits for tax purposes. Also, as you grow older, your tax will probably become less. The plan we have worked out gives you an option as to when you want to pay taxes on that interest.

Personally, I like that trust fund idea for other things as well. For example, take a portfolio of stocks. Some stocks are always going up and some down, but, by occasionally adding up the value of your entire lot, you come to a much better appraisal of how you are doing. Such a procedure likewise avoids that uncomfortable feeling when you take a loss. You look at the whole thing more objectively and become a trustee paying yourself income.

The solution of a much more complex problem was worked out by officers of the Teachers Insurance and Annuity Association, which got its start through a grant from the Carnegie Corporation. Thousands of professors and their college employers had taken out annuities with the association. They liked the idea of annuities because of the guaranteed life income. But, in recent years, there has been a bad feature to consider. Interest rates have been so low on conservative investments that the annuity holder has had to have a great deal of money invested in annuities in order to have much income. And, besides, that small income buys so little at the corner grocery.

The Teachers Insurance and Annuity Association wondered how it would be possible to adapt the principle of investment in common stocks to annuity holdings. That obviously presented quite a problem. The market value and dividends of common stocks fluctuate from year to year. But, over a long, long period of years, many of the better stocks have shown substantial dividend yields as well as increases in value. So the officers of the association saw an advantage in setting up a separate corporation and permitting annuity buyers to accumulate one-half of their annuity in common stocks and one-half in the old-time bonds.

But how are you going to guarantee a yearly annuity when the cash values back of it are constantly fluctuating? It is easy enough, of course, to pay the income, as a trust fund, but how are you to apportion things year by year so that the capital as well as the income will be used up in an average lifetime?

The problem was solved by changing the dollar values to unit values. A man makes his payments into the fund on the basis of units, representing a portion of the stocks owned at the prevailing value. The units may cost ten dollars each at one time, or fifteen dollars, or five dollars, depending on the market value of the total. When it comes to paying him back his stock investment over a long period of years, he is paid in units. If, each year, he should be receiving 8 per cent, based on his life expectancy, he would be given eight units out of each hundred that he originally owned. These units are to be immediately converted into dollars based on the value of the units in the fund at the time. Of course it is expected that over a long period of years the units will develop extra value as the stocks behind them increase.

What else comes to mind when we think of annuities and their possibilities? Naturally, guaranteed income for life has considerable popularity as a supplement to social security. Does anyone see how the government might help solve one of its own problems by making use of the annuity principle? Some reader probably pictures the government offering the individual holders of its bonds the option of turning them in for an annuity. That might add a great deal to the popularity of government bonds and at the same time extend the maturity of the government debt.

Help When You're Helpless

There are always problems remaining in this world, but there is a universal one that faces small manufacturers and

[145]

inventors in the fields of science or mechanics. What do you do when you are up a tree and don't know what to do? We have our idea started, but it does not seem to "jell." Our chemical formula ought to work but does not. Some underlying principle baffles us. Maybe we have the wrong materials. A calculating machine won't help there. The whole thing seems beyond us.

We are not General Electric, DuPont, or RCA. We cannot afford million-dollar laboratories and a staff of scientists. Problems are more complicated than ever before in this twentieth century, but, at the same time, the small corporation has more ways of getting help than ever before.

It simply farms out the problem to a research laboratory and, in due course, receives the answer. The fee may run from a thousand dollars on up to many, many times that sum. Even universities accept problems from corporations and put graduate students at work checking possible solutions.

One of the most famous of such laboratories is the nonprofit Battelle Memorial Institute at Columbus, Ohio. In about 25 years it has grown from an institution employing 20 men to one now employing about 2,000. It is equipped to tackle almost any scientific problem. For instance, the Elgin National Watch Company sponsored a research project at Battelle to secure its nonmagnetic watch spring. The Haloid Company had its "dry printing" device developed there. When no one wanted copper years ago, the great copper corporations put it up to the institute to find new markets. Before long, the institute had the basic work done on such interesting things as a ship's paint that keeps barnacles off and the addition of copper elements to fertilizer to raise tobacco yields and to road materials to prevent roads from cracking when laid in wet weather.

And so, problems go on forever. There is an interesting thing, however, about creative solutions in life and business. There are many solutions, more than for problems in mere mathematics. There are many ways to accomplish the same basic end. There are many trains one might take on many different railroads, and yet one would arrive at the same destination. There are thousands of places for a vacation, and yet they have the same basic end—having a good time. I have often thought what fun it would be to take the clerks and store officials from Tiffany's, Woolworth's, and Neiman-Marcus and mix them all up in a new store. It would be interesting, to say the least. These stores are all different and have their own methods, but their one ultimate end is to sell more goods. They all proceed in different directions and travel on different trains but arrive at the same place—sales.

Finally, if you can't solve your problem, maybe you can go around it. This is indeed a highly successful way of solving the problem. Do you know where sports journalism originated? Years ago, Victor Murdock, who became one of the great Kansas editors, was working for a Chicago newspaper. He was sent out to cover a baseball game. He did not know too much about the intricacies of baseball, so when he returned, he resorted to the trick of writing a funny story about it. It made a hit. Sports writing, where you could depart from the customary style of journalism, was on the way.

Next time a problem faces *you,* try a creative solution.

{11

Getting the Best of the Past

The Arab looked at the stars. "Maybe a hundred, maybe a thousand years ago," he remarked. "Time does not matter."

Thus did the Arab suggest the magnitude of the past. I like the past. I like its vastness. I like to think of the thousands of generations running back to the beginning of time. It is like standing on top of Pike's Peak and gazing through limitless space. It is as if we had lifted the horizon itself. Here a similarity between time and space becomes evident, because looking backwards in time, we can see such a distance. We can see so many things.

The remarkable point, of course, is that the higher we go up a mountain or in an airplane the more we see laid out before us. The minor details of the landscape may become blurred. The farmers' grain elevator that looms so high over

Smithville when we are on the ground can hardly be seen at all. Instead, we see other things—mountains, forests, prairies, and great rivers.

The farther we progress along the great path of time and the older we are, the greater perspective we have looking backwards. We see events as well as incidents, great forces as well as matters of the moment. The older man and woman get quite a break here.

The past should be of more benefit than it usually is in the great field of creation. With more and more past on which to build, civilization should grow better, happier, wiser. The further we go in civilization, the easier and more pleasant life should become.

When you stop to think of it, the past is the basis of the development of the individual and the world. The difficulty is that education is seldom directed to the creative utilization of the past in the living present.

I was thinking it over. "What practical good are the years gone by?" I asked myself. "How can we do more with the past?" And then I thought, "Let's ask other people what they take out of it."

There was a great university at hand. Education, I recalled, is always giving people airplane rides over the past. "Let's ask the professors," I said to myself. So I began.

The professor of languages, whose books are used in many colleges, put me in the big lounge chair in his office. "It's funny, maybe, but the older I get, the more I find myself thinking in the past," he remarked. "Not just my own past but the whole past of history. It's great fun to let your mind run backwards. Why? Here's my answer. The past can't hurt me now. I can enjoy all the battles and the adventures without danger of cracking a fingernail."

In part, the professor of sociology agreed. "Many of us use the past as something of a sedative. Not only when things are unpleasant do we take refuge in the past, but we actually select the past we want and try to begin living in time.

"But there is another important point," he continued. "Until you know the past, you don't appreciate our present. 'The ancients have stolen all our good ideas,' as someone has said."

The psychologist was interested, so interested, in fact, that he proposed that all the professors be interviewed and their ideas tabulated. I would find out whether a scientist got more out of the past than a sociologist, whether a chemist showed more appreciation than a physicist.

"Frankly, I believe that few people actually make use of the past beyond their own personal acquaintance with it," he said. "My own father knew seven generations, from his great-grandparents to the great-grandchildren. Because of his age, he had personal experience with time. But I doubt if he ever went much beyond those experiences."

The professor of literature had a different answer for me: "I see men walking up and down in the great past, men who had destiny and faith within their grasp, dynamic figures that were to mean something to the future. They are examples for the present."

The professor of chemistry, strangely enough, reminded me of the professor of literature. "I derive inspiration from the many great men who make up history. The achievements of others in their time and surroundings make anything most of us do seem commonplace. They keep one from conceit."

The president of the university saw in the great past the "moving and enduring forces in time." The difficulty with so many books of history, he thought, is that detail obscures the subject. "We see only incidents rather than great forces."

"We learn or should learn something from the experiences of predecessors who faced the same problems as we," asserted the classical scholar. "Much the same social and economic problems have always existed. The past should enable us to avoid mistakes in the present."

I found a great buyer of solid books down the street. He is different from the professors who get most of their books at the library. This man is in the market for almost any set of "classics" bound in half morocco.

"I'm not sure history contributes to my enjoyment of life," he said. "We spend a lot of time searching for frills rather than real living. The ancients did not have to purchase a late-model automobile to horrify or tickle them. They were more interested in fundamentals."

"Maybe they had to be," I put in.

Well, what do you think of the professors? I think they are like all of us. They use the past for creative purposes, but do not make a regular practice of it.

Most of us do not have a clear idea of just what we want from the past. But, once we understand the purpose of what we are doing, we may, I think, walk up and down the past with more benefit to ourselves.

We Go Prospecting in the Past

When the present becomes irksome we try to get away from it. Those who can afford it pack up for Nassau or Sun

Valley. But most of us are like the professors who have to use the past for their swimming and skiing. We get out the books and read unless we have a television set. We like to talk with friends about the past or sometimes just remember by ourselves. "We remember things as we would have liked to have had them," A. W. Grant, San Antonio editor, remarked one day to me. Each day we would escape the present by creating a new old world of things better than they really were.

But why not a new present instead? Our own present and the present of the world should be a lot better because both we and the world have had a past.

The past is something like a great forest. Did you ever get lost in a forest? That produces an eerie feeling when you see about you all sorts of little open places that look as if they might be the beginning of paths. And where do the footprints go?

I once visited the Crocker Art Gallery in Sacramento. Judge E. B. Crocker spent the years 1868–1870 in Europe, and, when he arrived home, he brought a collection of art with him. He did not bring home just a few paintings; some people said he bought a museum full and had it shipped home.

The so-called big things in his collection did not prove to be as important as had once been thought. But, years later, down in the basement of the house, were discovered stacks of pictures forgotten for half a century. There were 1,000 drawings from the hands of old masters from the fifteenth to the nineteenth centuries. The prize of the collection was a study by Albrecht Dürer, perhaps a preparatory sketch for an engraving, "The Dream." It alone was valued well up in the thousands of dollars.

But now you ask me: "Did you ever know of a person who dug up a prize idea while exploring the past?"

And I answer, "Yes." Idea diamonds have been found by going back to prehistoric times as well as by going back only to the pasts of our own fathers.

The great past runs back of our recorded history, so far back that we see only the results of it in the creation of the world. "Our job," remarked Willard H. Dow, the great industrial chemist, "is with infinite patience to work out the great laws of nature and then find a way to direct the workings of those natural laws into channels where they may serve mankind."

Our Department of Defense is making use of the prehistoric past. One of these days we may have a war in the Arctic. The possibilities of mining and oil treasures suggest that the northern part of America may have more and more settlers. So Army engineers are working on the great question: "How do you build things up there?" They maintain a line of investigation called SIPRE, or the Snow, Ice and Permafrost Research Establishment.

It appears that we might have saved ourselves a great deal of trouble in building the Alcan and other highways in the far north. By spreading gravel and building materials on top of the natural vegetable insulation, we introduced a substance that had a high heat conductivity; the result was that the ice tended to thaw beneath the roads.

So now we think about doing it as nature does it. Ice and snow are being studied as building materials, particularly ice that is about 10,000 years old. At 65 degrees below zero it is as hard as limestone.

Powdered metal is now being used in making metal parts

at a saving of up to 50 per cent of the usual cost. The metal is first turned to powder, then pressed under heavy weights and baked into its final shape. Where did the idea originate? It is based upon a process used by the Egyptians before the days of Christ.

René Laënnec was listening to the intermediate past when he devised the stethoscope. A young woman patient was unusually stout and at the same time very modest. He felt that she would be disconcerted if he put his ear directly to her chest, but her stoutness prevented his learning anything by tapping it. Then he had his idea.

"I happened to recollect," he wrote afterward, "a simple and well-known fact in acoustics, and fancied it might be turned to some use on the present occasion. The fact I allude to is the great distinctness with which we hear the scratch of a pin at one end of a piece of wood, on applying our ear to the other. Immediately, on this suggestion, I rolled a quire of paper into a kind of cylinder and applied one end of it to the region of the heart and the other to my ear, and was not a little surprised and pleased, to find that I could thereby perceive the action of the heart in a manner much more clear and distinct than I had ever been able to do by the immediate application of the ear. From this moment I imagined that the circumstance might furnish means for enabling us to ascertain the character, not only of the action of the heart, but of every species of sound produced by the motion of the thoracic viscera. . . . With this conviction I forthwith commenced at the Hospital Necker a series of observations from which I have been able to deduce a set of new signs of diseases of the chest."

Our great drug manufacturers and medical laboratories

take a look at some of the old remedies of the Indians, Chinese, and other races. Mandrake, an old Indian remedy for stomach trouble, seems, for instance, to have a retarding effect on cancer. There was often, in the past, the right action for the wrong reason. During the days of the hideous yellow fever epidemics, great fires of pitch were kindled on the street corners in the belief that they prevented the disease. Probably they did, for what wandering mosquito would want to stay around in that smudge?

If some person, looking about Europe years ago, had been "on the beam," he might have gone down as the discoverer of penicillin. For there were those housewives slapping a piece of mouldy bread on a wound. It was the forerunner of the great principle of antibiotics of the present day. But no one asked, "Why?"

In the chemical field, over half a million compounds have been put together, and the number is growing at the rate of more than 30,000 a year. The question arises as to how many great medical and other blessings for the world exist this very minute in some unappreciated compound. Sulfanilamide was first manufactured as a dye-industry chemical in 1908. But it was an entire quarter century before Gerhard Domagk saw the wonderful medical properties of sulfa drugs.

Dr. Benjamin Miller of Boston has suggested the interesting thought that all of the existing drugs and chemical compounds might well be screened against the possibility that we have a cancer cure and do not know it. But Robert Barney, a writer on cancer, says that we already have hundreds of chemical compounds that give indications of curing

[155]

cancer but poison the patient. The problem, he thinks, is to work forward and try to make these drugs nontoxic.

The exploration of the past should be a strange and wonderful experience. It is, for the scientist, the inventor, and even the businessman and artist, something like going into a far country. So many things have happened or almost happened that should be productive of thought today. As Williams Haynes so aptly remarked: "Hundreds of patents have expired without being successfully commercialized simply because they came before their time. They failed to catch that tide that leads on to fortune."

The businessman will usually concern himself with the more immediate past. Looking back over his own lifetime, he will recall many things that almost made the grade but had to wait a number of years before they came into general acceptance. Today airbrakes are common on buses and trucks. Yet I can remember when one venturesome manufacturer provided his passenger car with such brakes plus a source of compressed air for pumping up one's own tires. It was the old Northern automobile.

Sports-style automobiles have been growing in popularity in recent years; yet older men and women recall the day when sports cars *were* sports cars—lavish cars with the names of Stutz and Jordan. Travelers in California 30 years ago will recall buses with a degree of luxury not attained today. They had lavatories; they served meals; they had smoking and parlor sections, and even an observation platform! Maybe, one of these days, bus companies will go back and take a look at what was on the road then.

Robert Rhea in Colorado Springs stepped back and made the Dow-Jones theory a profitable background for a financial forecasting service. The Dow theory was put forth around the turn of the century by Charles H. Dow, as a means of determining whether the stock market was in an ascending or descending cycle. The theory had lain dormant in later years until Robert Rhea, who had been studying its scope, stepped into the forecasting picture.

The past seems to play a greater part in the life of the architect and the clothes designer than that of the average businessman. First, this is because modern-day business is comparatively new. The second point is that, in art, we tend to respect the past. If you doubt this, ask the price of a Rembrandt or a Rubens. Such reverence for the past has always been evident in architecture as demonstrated by the number of public buildings whose style is that of Greece or Rome.

The businessman turns this feeling for the past to practical account by marketing things based on the traditions of the past. The field of adaptation in women's clothes is full of the styles of the past worked into the present. Wallpaper and textiles borrow designs from the past. And there is your dear wife—all steamed up over those magic names of Sheraton, Hepplewhite, and Chippendale. Unless she has become a convert to modernism, she is going to get out your check-book!

Practical Uses of the Past

What suggestions do we have for making use of the past?

1. Do not become a slave to the past. Do not dissipate all your energy resting up in the past as an escape from an unhappy present. Moderate doses of the past are recreation. The past should be an adventure, once in a while, not a

constant absorption. Many students and scholars go through life taking one college course after another, one graduate fellowship after another, and yet never make any creative contribution to civilization. Remember that the main direction in life is always forward.

2. When you do rest up in the past, either by reading or conversation, learn to pick up the ideas that are really valuable to you. Treat the past the same as travel. Many businessmen travel with the idea of seeing "what's going on." Do the same with books. "The library! What a dull name for one of the most enchanting places in the world," exclaims Herman U. Leedy. "Dig in it. Much will be dull, drab, and uninteresting. But keep digging. Here and there you will find mental gold, silver, and precious stones."

You draw upon the past in relating it to the present. The simplest illustration of this is in going through a desk or filing cabinet. You find all sorts of papers, things that you had forgotten existed. You pull out something, look it over and say to yourself, "Here's just the idea I need for today." And you take it and use it. If you have a good memory, you may do the same with the stores of the mind. That is one reason why we suggest that you keep a notebook of your own ideas.

3. The immediate past is, of course, generally of greater significance than the far past because its ideas are more closely related to the present and the adaptation can be easily accomplished. For example, the Minnesota highway department borrowed an idea from World War II, when magnets were used to clear airstrips of bits of metal sowed there by the Nazis to puncture the tires of landing planes. Why not use something of the kind to clear the metal off

Minnesota highways? So there are trucks that gather up metal by means of magnets. As much as 600 pounds are picked up in a 75-mile trip.

4. Naturally, it will be of more value for you to read and study in your own field rather than simply enjoy general reading. "A disability under which the non-professional inventor works is a lack of knowledge of the prior art," says L. S. Hardland of the National Inventors Council. "He often does not know even in a general way what has been tried and discarded or tried, patented, and put into use. Because he has not seen it himself, he feels that it does not exist, and shaking this conviction is sometimes very difficult." Procter & Gamble, whose libraries contain 17,000 volumes, one of the largest and most complete collections of material on soaps, synthetic detergents, and shortenings to be found anywhere, points out, "No scientist can even begin without knowing what has already been done."

5. But once you have your idea in hand, move forward with it into the present and future by the process we have previously indicated. The trouble is that many people never move forward, they just stay in the past.

The Profitable Art of Being Contrary

What else? Yes, there is another great use of the past. Here you do not pick up only an idea of "what to do" but also "how to do." What caused things to turn out the way they did in the past? Hugh Bancroft, famous publisher of many financial periodicals, was some years ago extolling to me the outstanding qualities of a good reporter. "One reporter comes in and writes that 'The Easy-Haul Railroad

Company today passed its dividend,'" he told me. "But not Bill. He could say he had predicted it. That passing of the dividend was simply an outgrowth of what Bill had seen all along. He had told his readers long ago what was bound to happen." Men in finance know that you have to have facts out of the past in order to judge the present.

Just before the panic of 1929, John Flynn, in a remarkable article in the *American Magazine,* dug up that little rhyme of long ago:

> "On Monday I bought share on share,
> On Tuesday I was a millionaire;
> On Wednesday I took a grand abode,
> On Thursday in my carriage rode;
> On Friday went to the opera hall;
> On Saturday came to the pauper's hall."

That little poem had been written some 200 years before when the Mississippi Bubble had burst in France. Mr. Flynn warned of the same possibility in 1929. No one can say that he was not using his knowledge and research into the past.

George Shea, famous for his financial analysis in *Barron's* and the *Wall Street Journal,* has called attention, as a result of his observation of the past, to the serious situation that arises when credit is still expanding but commodity prices are falling. Then it is time to be careful. If inflation can't make prices go up, look out!

Some say that all hear the voice of experience, but plenty of people have not been listening very well the past few decades. What an ado we made when Japan attacked us without warning at Pearl Harbor! Certainly few of our government leaders could have been looking into the past because that was simply generally recognized Japanese procedure. If you are going to have a war, why bother saying so? Isn't starting a war notice enough? That was standard Japanese thinking. It was in the books. Even A. L. Gump, San Francisco businessman, wrote a letter to the White House months before calling attention to that very dangerous situation, as he had observed it.

Stalin certainly had a bad enough reputation after having sent millions into slavery; yet an American reference book referred to him as "a great statesman."

And Hitler! So negligent of the past was the president of a small college that he proclaimed, as a reporter friend told me, that "Hitler is my model." And countless people in the world began booting each other around, entranced by Hitler's example.

Do people read history? If so, do they remember things out of it, or do they remember only a mass of dates? When one looks back over the past three decades, one wonders how much was really being learned in school.

The sum total of the past is always exhibiting itself in the present as experience. But some did not learn their lesson. The experience we have had may have been good or bad. Strangely enough, really good experience may have been a series of mistakes that we do not propose making a second time. Often we have failed to build on a particular mistake. To profit by the past is the easiest and most valuable way to relate to the present an unhappy incident of the past. I have known many individuals who have lost positions or suffered bankruptcy and who have immediately started out on new work so successfully that they look back on the events of the past as having been the best things that could possibly have happened to them.

"Well, I won't make that mistake again," we find ourselves saying.

And that brings us to something of great significance—the profitable art of being contrary. The big thing I get out of the past is the need for and the desirability of contrary thinking. The use of such thinking is in itself creative and has been capitalized in a realistic way by Humphrey Neill in his *Letters of Contrary Opinion* which, published in Saxtons River, Vermont, have attained a great vogue among business executives.

The idea back of such thinking is the realization that most people are selling stocks when they should be buying them, buying stocks when they should be selling, building up inventories when they should be cutting down, cutting down when they should be building them up, going into business when they should be getting out, and getting out when they should be getting in. If you do the wrong thing more than half the time, you will be sunk, financially or otherwise. "Unless we are wiser today than yesterday we must expect to fail tomorrow" are the memorable words of Carl Holmes.

There is, of course, real reason for the contrary action being more successful than the one most people are following at the moment. When everyone has been buying stocks and has loaded up at high prices with no more money to invest, stocks will likely go down. But when there are ample funds and everything is dirt cheap, good stocks will sooner or later advance.

When people are in a storm cellar, the tornado does not

harm them. When they are prepared for a panic, a panic re-
fuses to put in an appearance.

There is an interesting point involved here. If nearly
everyone became "contrary minded" so to speak, then only
"contra-contrary-minded" people or maybe the dumb ones
would profit by doing the opposite of what the contrary-
minded people did. Mr. Neill suggests this: "Just before
World War II ended government economists predicted a se-
vere postwar depression of the magnitude of 1921. . . .
'Everyone' remembered (or had read about) the collapse in
1920–21, following the first world war. People jumped to
the conclusion that 'it would be the same this time.' As we
now know, it was quite different. There was no slump.

"However, this idea of a postwar recession became a fixa-
tion in people's minds. All during the years 1946, 1947, 1948
and 1949, the thought of a 'recession' became an obsession.
The result was that business, being frightened and fearing a
sudden slump, played a conservative game. At the same time
the public's appetite for goods of all descriptions was so in-
tense that inflation set in and people spent money right and
left. The result: good business, indeed a boom, instead of the
'much advertised' recession."

In other words, the past may give you the wrong answer
when too many people are following what they believe to
be the lesson of the past. You often read in financial circulars of the tremendous sums one might have made by purchasing a certain stock years before. But that does not neces-
sarily mean that the same success will be achieved in that
stock in the future.

During the drouth and depression years of the thirties a
man created a sensation in a western town. He was not in-

[163]

hibited by the thinking of ordinary people. He was a contrary thinker when no one else was contrary. One day, he suddenly appeared and went from one real estate man to another and from banker to banker inquiring of each what distress property was for sale. "Yes, I guess I'll take that piece," he would say, "and that other one too. Wrap up that business block also." Going here, there, and everywhere, he bought up nearly every piece of property that was on the market in that town.

Then it was discovered that he didn't have any money with which to buy. It was decided that he was unbalanced and they put him in a mental hospital. "Funny thing, isn't it?" remarked the banker some years later when everything was booming in the town and prices of property were sky high. "They've got him in the asylum for having the right idea, and they are letting the rest of us who couldn't think straight run around loose."

"The past is dead!" we may exclaim.

But then we hastily add, "Long live the past!"

And it keeps on living whether we manage it our way or not.

"Time does not matter," said the Arab. But he might have added, "It is what happens that counts."

To different people this chapter may suggest different things. To the businessmen it may suggest the many opportunities for building on ideas of the past as well as the value of contrary thinking; to the student and teacher it may suggest that a different approach to education may be needed, to the government official that the reputations of countries and individuals are usually written in the past.

$\{12$

Energizing Yourself

ON A GOLDEN AUTUMN AFTERNOON many years ago a distinguished white-haired gentleman picked up his pen and wrote on the page before him:

He can who thinks he can

A youngster—myself—had asked him, sitting there in his office on New York's lower Fifth Avenue, the most significant thing he had learned after having served as the inspiration of millions of young businessmen for a generation.

Where a writer of the present day might consider himself lucky to sell 20,000 copies of a book, he would sell 100,000; where 200,000 would be big business today, he would sell a million. He had several college degrees but had been a hotel man, having been initiated into that field as a youth when he waited table summers with Frank A. Munsey up in the White Mountains.

At the Midway Hotel in Kearney, Nebraska, he had been writing a book, *Pushing to the Front*. But one night the hotel burned to the ground and with it the manuscript of the book. A ruined man, he rented a room over the livery stable, lived on $1.50 a week, and rewrote the book.

Not long after, Queen Victoria and other great figures of the day were giving his work their endorsements, and the book was being translated into a score of languages.

His name was Orison Swett Marden and, in the closing years of his life, he put down for me the summation of what he had learned after writing some 40 books of inspiration which had become the success bibles of countless young men.

Every once in a while, a person looking at this matter of creative thought says, "I agree perfectly with everything you say, but I have a feeling there is something else to be added." Marden expressed what they mean by "the something else." Many times, writers have dealt with the means of energizing themselves rather than the great basic process which we have aimed to develop in this volume. Getting up steam is important.

The Three Greats

I do not suppose there are many reading these lines who expect to become great prophets, great benefactors of humanity, great inventors—men and women who are to belong to the ages rather than to the present. But there may be some. The strange thing is that at the present moment they probably have not the slightest inkling that their names are going to live in the years to come. For the magic future elevates many of low position and removes the mighty from their thrones.

But there are three great things that have much to do with developing such men and women and indeed something to do with supplying us with energy for our more ordinary creations. They are:

The Great Cause
The Great Inspiration
The Great Confidence

Life seems to demand a philosophy. Believe, believe, believe in something, and we never seem quite satisfied until we have done so. Every businessman will tell you what his faith in an idea—his idea—has done for him. When we no longer have faith in ourselves, in others, or in some great religious or philosophical idea, we seem to go to pieces.

Salt Lake City was and is a city of faith, as much a city of faith as those cities I have seen in distant parts of the world. One Sunday afternoon, I ventured over to the Tabernacle to hear its great music. But it was more than an ordinary occasion. For it had just been decided that one of the organists who played the great Tabernacle instrument should go to Germany to take charge of the Mormon missionary work there. And he was making his speech of acceptance, as it were. I wondered what kind of speech I'd be making if the old Presbyterian church back home had just decided to send me off somewhere. Probably I would have found plenty of reasons for staying right at home. But to this man, making his speech of acceptance, it was the greatest honor in the world; there could be no greater.

Most figures of history have felt that they were serving in great causes. St. Paul felt the great cause. St. Francis felt it. Abraham Lincoln felt it. So did Patrick Henry. Florence Nightingale was sure of hers. Albert Schweitzer, great organist and philosopher, feels the great cause today as a missionary-physician in Africa. Robert E. Lee felt the cause. Thousands in history acted the way they did because of a cause. You may not agree with the cause, but from their point of view it was tremendously important. Unless they had been engaged in a great cause, they would not have become great figures.

The businessman often feels that he is laboring for a great cause right in his own office. Rotary, Kiwanis, and Lions Clubs and all the rest have for part of their philosophy that the ordinary man should work to make civilization better.

John Wanamaker felt that he was in a great cause. His job was more than running a department store, more than simply selling things. It was to create a center of great music for everyone, art in everyday life, better employee relations, and better opportunities for employees. The store was to be a palace as well as a market. Timothy and Sir John Eaton had a similar vision of storekeeping in Canada.

J. C. Penney told me one day that he thought the most potent reason for his success in the early years of his chain was the unusual way in which he was able at that time to give the young managers of his first stores an opportunity to obtain an interest in the business. In fact, Penney was one of the pioneers in profit sharing as well as in the business of doing good.

[168]

After a man had some experience with him and began to show promise, Penney would pick him as the manager of a new store. He received a third interest in that store. After a while, that store prospered and made enough money so that it could finance a second store. A new man was started out with a third interest, but the manager of the store that had financed it had a third interest also. Soon that second store could start a third with its profits and another young man was given a third interest. Each of the managers of the two "father" stores had a third interest. But, as this third store prospered and branched out, the manager of the first store was eliminated from further ownership in that direction in order to make room for someone else.

But, in the meantime, the first store had been making money and might have started a couple of other offshoot stores in other directions with the original manager having third interests in them. The final result was that many men gradually acquired third interests in many stores. They found themselves with snug fortunes. Now and then you will run across old "J. C. Penney millionaires."

Undoubtedly much of the success that DeWitt Wallace achieved with the *Reader's Digest* was due to the touch of idealism and the better life that he endeavored to inculcate in the lives of Americans. I remember a long luncheon session and an hour or two afterward in the lounge of a New York hotel when he labored diligently to convert me to the possibilities of helping remake American life by the idea route. One could see that Wallace was and is in many ways a crusader. He could preach. "Churches, schools, and government—they all need ideas," he asserted.

So we come to that second point, the great inspiration.

Did you ever hear a great lecture and go home all warmed up with new energy for your task? Did you have a favorite school teacher who started you off to make a name for yourself? Or do you have friends that radiate inspiration?

Through friends and acquaintances we become interested in many things, and our ideas tend to take form according to these interests. It is hard to create where we have no interest.

Few have equalled the inspiration of Russell H. Conwell, lawyer, army officer, journalist, and preacher. His great lecture, *Acres of Diamonds,* was delivered several thousand times. When a great anniversary lecture-celebration was held in Philadelphia for the 5,000th delivery of the lecture, over $9,000 was taken in at the Academy of Music. Like the great figures of history, Dr. Conwell had a cause. Inspired by his own struggles at Yale, he devoted the hundreds of thousands of dollars he took in from the lecture to helping poor boys through school. He was the founder of Temple University.

The lecture itself received its title from a story an Arab guide told Dr. Conwell when he was going down the Tigris and Euphrates rivers. It was the story of a man who became possessed of the diamond fever, sold his farm, and wandered over the earth in search of diamonds until, finally, impoverished and discouraged, he took his own life. Another man purchased his old farm and found therein the great diamond mines of Golconda.

The moral was obvious, and Dr. Conwell kept telling the story and all its implications for many years, each time fitting the story to the city in which he happened to be. A very strange thing happened one day, a great incident that Dr.

Conwell could add to his later lectures. In New Britain, Connecticut, a woman and her husband had attended the lecture; on returning home, the lady tried to take off her collar, but the button would not budge (apparently the woman used collar buttons!). The husband chided his wife: "After what Conwell said tonight, you see there is a need of an improved collar button. There is a human need and a great fortune to be found. Now then, get up a new collar button and get rich." And his wife did get up a new collar button. She did not stop at this one button but invented several others and became a partner in great companies. So rich did she become, as Dr. Conwell attests, that she punished her unbelieving husband by making him go to Europe every year on her private yacht.

The great inspirer of the present day is Norman Vincent Peale, who manages to stay well on the top of the best-seller list. Almost automatically Peale's inspiration brings us to that next point, the great confidence. "Believe in yourself!" urges Dr. Peale. "Have faith in your abilities! Without a humble but reasonable confidence in your own powers you cannot be successful or happy. But with sound self-confidence you can succeed. A sense of inferiority and inadequacy interferes with the attainment of your hopes, but self-confidence leads to self-realization and successful achievement."

Why do so many successful men become more and more successful? It is not entirely a matter of money but rather the fact that success breeds confidence and the more confidence one has, the more ideas come along. Did you ever sell things? Perhaps you had a discouraging day, and it seemed nothing good would come out of it. But, about three-thirty, you made a sale and, strangely enough, from that moment on, you made three or four sales right in succession. I'll wager that a great deal of the reason back of it is that you radiated confidence.

Some of you may remember the National Cash Register salesmen of a generation ago. As a boy, I watched the man in our town with great awe, walking almost at a run from store to store, as apparently he had been taught to do. Successful salesmen today still radiate success, but they are more likely to drive up in a Cadillac.

Now we get down to earth!

What do I, you want to know, make of all this?

To begin with, we must point out that great causes, great inspiration and great confidence are not substitutes for the process of creation. They may, however, activate it tremendously without our being aware of what is going on.

The men of this chapter make us feel that we can do it, too. This adds up to the significant fact that plenty of people in this world have plenty of ability if they would but use it. What Marden, Conwell, and Peale have been saying is to make the most of ourselves. Thousands of people have their tonsils out, their adenoids out, and their teeth out, but few have all possible ideas extracted from their heads.

Nothing delights a teacher more than to see some young man who did not do so well in school winning his real spurs out in the world. I run across such individuals every now and then. They are not all sitting in the seats of the mighty, but they are making comfortable livings and raising happy families. Once in a while they ask what to do with their surplus money; so everything must be all right.

And here is a suggestion to teachers, parents, and employers. Encouragement and praise are worth five times as much as all the fault finding and grumbling one can muster. Just suppose Marden, Conwell, and Peale had been going around this world telling everyone that the world was finished and each individual bound to be a failure.

Would you and your fathers have listened to them?

Now finally you ask me, "Where did Orison Swett Marden, with whom you began this chapter, get the idea of producing his memorable book, *Pushing to the Front?*"

It was an idea derived strictly in accord with the principles we have been laying down in this work: from Samuel Smiles' *Self-Help* published in England, as Marden himself once told me. Marden aimed to do for the United States what Smiles had done for England. And soon Marden was selling his own books in England.

I conclude this chapter purposely with that note in order to show that even the inspirers use the basic principle we have laid down in this book—that every idea starts from something else. Inspiration supplements and makes us want to pursue that idea to its final successful conclusion.

{13

How to Make Ideas Sneak Up On You

A GOOD MANY YEARS AGO there was one common view about creative thinking—that a bright idea came like a streak of lightning and a clap of thunder. But no one explained precisely how.

Later, there was another widely praised technique of creative thinking. You simply went to sleep and awakened in the middle of the night with a million-dollar idea.

But the trouble with the first notion was that the lightning did not strike many people. And the second offered too great a temptation. Thousands of people were tired and sleepy, and this technique was just too good to be true. Not having experienced the clap of thunder, they decided to take a nap. They had a good snooze, but 99.99 per cent of them did not get their million-dollar ideas.

Some people just aren't satisfied with ordinary ways of

doing things. They want magic. It is natural that anyone should desire a big idea without any work at all. Even the United States Supreme Court declared that an invention is a "flash of Genius—an instantaneous solution." But thousands of successful inventors who have slaved and sweated in cellar and garage would probably hand down quite a contrary decision to that of the Supreme Court.

It is true that people have had sudden bright ideas come to them. It is true that people have awakened in the night with bright solutions to problems.

But why did not the other 99.99 per cent have bright ideas come to them suddenly by night or day?

The answer is quite obvious, I think. They had made no preparation for the big ideas and were not ready to receive them.

The Efficient Creator

How do you quicken this discovery process? How do you make the mind work faster at the job? How do you get up steam, so to speak?

"I don't feel quite up to par today." How often have you heard that? Tens of thousands of people are saying it today, said it yesterday, and will say it tomorrow.

A young man on the street just told me this: "I'm so tired when evening comes I just can't do anything extra." Maybe you have heard that before.

I presume most people run at only 25 per cent mental efficiency and rarely accomplish a fraction of what they might. The tragedy of life is not lack of brain power or education but doing so little with what we have. A great deal of this is caused by lack of knowledge of how to go about securing and developing ideas. But part of it is also due to the fact that, as people say, they "can't pull one foot ahead of the other."

Anyone who has had contact with large numbers of students realizes that an unusually large proportion are not quite up to the struggle. Plenty of people in offices and stores feel the same way. The number of young people who are defeated not only in colleges but also in life by this "down and out feeling" is very large. Everyone has it to some extent, but, with many, it is almost a chronic disease.

Older people may feel this way more than young ones. Theoretically, older people, with more background upon which to draw, should be more creative than young people. But youth has won a reputation for being creative largely because it has more get-up-and-go to pursue adaptations and see them through to success.

Yet, if these less efficient people went to a doctor, he would probably find nothing seriously wrong. But they haven't much get-up, and it may be that much of that feeling comes from a vitamin and mineral deficiency. Undoubtedly one of the great contributions to well-being during the past two decades has been the increasing knowledge of nutrition. Ask your own doctor about how you can be helped by this new knowledge.

But there is another kind of fatigue. A Michigan personnel man asked an employee why he stayed home so much and whether or not he was sick. "Well," answered the man, "sometimes I am sick at the stomach but sometimes I am sick of the job, and then I stay home, too."

Yes, fatigue, particularly mental fatigue, may be due to

the fact that you are just sick and tired of what you are doing. This is often true when you are pursuing a single idea. You cannot force yourself to dig up ideas just as you cannot drive yourself to solve a problem. Your mind doesn't like that. Ideas must come easily and naturally. So when the idea search has you up a tree, assemble all the facts and material you can reasonably secure, stuff them into your head, and then go off and do something else.

Now, I am going to let you in on a little secret. It is just about as easy to keep three ideas going as one. Sir Isaac Newton's recreation consisted in changing from one subject to another. When he was tired of one thing and could not make progress with it, he laid it aside and tried something else for a few days. You can do the same thing. Let each project become a rest from the other project. Many times the mind will go on quietly working with the first project and deliver the answer to you later on quite as readily as if you had stayed with it every working minute.

Bess Streeter Aldrich, whose books sold hundreds of thousands of copies, told us one day that she would work on different chapters of a book all on the same day. When she got tired of one chapter, she simply turned to another.

But, when you are completely bogged down, you will have to take some time out to think. One day a letter came from a great corporation stating that it was having a hard time getting bright ideas out of its high-priced employees and wanting to know where the trouble might lie. I showed it to a learned friend. "Maybe they don't give them time to think," he remarked.

Often it is wise to get away from things, if you can. Later on, the ideas will begin to flow again. The mind seems to understand the task better than you and wants to work on it without too much conscious direction. Driving too hard may impede things. In my own case, I have been amazed how my mind picks up momentum just sitting on a railroad train amid new surroundings.

So, if you feel rusty about your project:

Do something different.

Read something outside your general experience.

Take some outdoor exercise or at least a walk.

See some new people.

Now, contrary as it may seem, it is important that your other activity take your conscious mind off the immediate matter that is bothering you. Outdoor exercise is always an aid to better feeling. Several years ago I used to take a horseback ride mornings and evenings. That compels you to take in oxygen. At the same time it pushes aside worries, for who can think about anything other than the unpredictable horse? Sports change your mental horizon. And they should be sports rather than the "up and down twenty times" which used to be so much in vogue in schools and colleges but which is now largely forgotten.

Of course, you may run across many direct ideas while you are doing other things, for the more things that come to your attention the more possible attributes you will observe. But you will also find your mind stimulated. Occasional change is a valuable aid to thought. Most thinking bends inward, and it is necessary to get out of the grooves of thought.

Our process of adaptation outlined in this book adds zest and makes resultful our reading, experiences, and travel. Mignon Good Eberhart, a famous mystery writer, made her big start while a hospital patient by writing *The Patient in*

Room 18 with a nurse as the detective. Her observation paid out handsomely.

When you are reading, let your mind travel and see what may be adapted from it. Does the success of the particular book in hand suggest that people are interested in that special subject? Does the merchandising success of one individual whose story you may be reading suggest that his plan might work with your business?

Or you may travel and pick up ideas all along the way. Sometimes it is exhilarating to take a business trip with no particular business in mind, paradoxical as that may sound. All you are setting out to do is to let things come to you. The great diamond fields of South Africa were discovered, it is said, because a man observed that the marbles with which some boys were playing were in reality crude diamonds.

All sorts of possibilities wait to be considered. As J. P. McEvoy of the *Reader's Digest* so aptly remarked: "Throw away your guidebook and follow an interest. Whether your passion is architecture or orchids, child welfare or rock gardens, fishing or folk dancing, butterflies or bridge, you will find devotees everywhere." But I would recommend that you go further than this and follow many interests, or better still, accumulate interests as you go along.

There is observation to be made even in the most unexpected places and of the simplest things. I was thinking about this one evening while cruising in the vicinity of Okinawa. Okinawa is noted for its gorgeous sunsets. But most Americans living there are unhappy, for they notice only the difficulties they encounter.

Here were our sunsets. There was a huge range of color

combinations constantly changing before my eyes. For the artist or designer the practical applications were many. How would "cloud pink" sound in advertising? What about some new dominant color for the artist seeking distinction? Remember what Dale Nichols did with blue?

Here you also saw how abrupt, clear-cut lines caused a cloud to stand out from the background. The sharper the lines the more the object seemed to come into the foreground.

You might have been an architect traveling with me. Here you would have seen an interesting terrace effect in the clouds that showed how apartments built up a steep hillside could utilize the roofs of the adjoining apartments below for outdoor terraces. You likewise would have seen the possibilities of irregular masses rather than regular ones. Everything in nature is not symmetrical; perhaps it is not necessary in man-made things. Worth thinking about?

You might have been a musician. Maybe the sight would have suggested to you a "Dance of the Clouds." Would you have made it rich, slow-moving, and sonorous, suggesting the huge billows of fleece, or would you have given it the fury of the whirlwind? Maybe you would have felt that it was an idea for a symphony, not just a little dance.

I do not mean that you should immediately step out and do the things I mention. I point them out as bits of observation from so simple a place as the rail of a slow-moving ship. More and more ideas pop up, happily enough, when you are just taking it easy.

Even conversation with other people is valuable and restful, particularly if you vary your companions. New friends are as worth while as new scenes in producing and remaking ideas.

That is why you find so many businessmen talking with one another in railway club cars. What did *you* learn today by the conversational route?

Sometimes the conversation may actually touch the very thing you have in mind, although you may not want to give away a really important idea to strangers unless you are sure of as good a one in return. That is a personal matter, however. Perhaps you are accumulating so many ideas which you never expect to use that you can afford to toss one into the air to see the reaction.

Alex Osborn, the advertising man, makes use of "brain-storming" as a means of idea production. It is conversation on the wholesale plan and, at the same time, co-operative idea creation. All participants are employees of the same company, and all are interested in its success; so the question of running off with another's idea does not matter. The whole thing is much like a college class in creative thinking. It starts with a basic problem, or perhaps one person hands out what seems to him like a bright idea. Then everyone else changes it around and adds to it, putting in a new attribute or keeping the attribute and supplying a new thing. Each participant thus enthuses the other. The entire venture may turn out quite differently indeed from anyone's expectations, but this simply illustrates the possibilities of creation.

An electrical engineer carrying on creative educational work with one of the great corporations told me that in a class it is not unusual to have 100 ideas from 15 students in half an hour's time. Warren L. Ganong, industrial engineer, had Friday afternoon classes in one corporation using the syllabus of the course I am expanding in this book. He found, over the entire company, that 42 per cent of all ideas suggested by employees were acceptable—a remarkable record.

This suggests an interesting possibility: the formation of an idea club. The club might belong to your school, company, or other organization. It would, of course, be run for fun, and its output might not be restricted to any one line. Since sessions would start without anything already created, participants would have nothing to lose.

The Snooze That Refreshes

Now we are going to let you take that snooze we warned against at the beginning of the chapter. If the lightning has not struck you standing up, it may well do so lying down. But it will do so only if you have been carrying out the suggestions we have made in this book. In other words, you have to feed the mind something on which to work.

After you have done what you can with the idea or problem, you say, figuratively, to the mind: "Here, Mind, take this in hand, and see what you can make of it." And, perhaps when you least expect it, you may experience the streak of lightning and clap of thunder and have the answer drop into your consciousness.

Men and women who have had sudden revelations, happened to be men and women who had been working at the task or a related task before. The mind simply went ahead at the problem or the observation and delivered the answer of its own accord. The ability of the mind to work without immediate direction seems to be too well established to be debatable.

Some people do secure their best ideas lying down. Edison used to take catnaps. Sir Walter Scott secured good ideas while reclining. Often the mind will deliver the answer to your problem in the middle of the night, or when you have just awakened in the morning. You will reach to the side table for a sheet of paper and pencil.

But, in using this procedure, don't get the worry habit and lie awake. Don't strain for midnight ideas. That is just the same as pushing your mind in the daytime. Let your mind alone at night, and let it do what it will. You may be surprised at some of the answers it will give you. But, more often, the answers will be in small pieces, supplementary ideas to use here and there. The great big smashing ideas are slower in coming, as one might expect.

But don't rush! Don't push! Creative thinking is not the New York subway.

{14

Play With Your Idea! Test It! Prove It!

Salvatore Gianola and Dominick Maglio, according to Navy reports, "almost died with their boots on, but because of them others will live."

"Would you go walking in a temperature of 42 degrees below zero with your boots filled with water to prove how good they are?" asks the Navy of its other personnel. "Would you go mountain climbing in New Hampshire in a frigid 25 degrees below zero, with winds of 100 miles per hour clawing at you to see how cold you get? Or perhaps you would rather feel the wind trying to blow you off the mountain with nothing but 3,000 feet of emptiness between you and certain death? Would you?"

I pass this nice little query along to those readers who are now ready to give their ideas a tryout. Salvatore Gianola and Dominick Maglio of Brooklyn invented a new type of boot designed to avoid those tragic losses suffered by army and navy men in cold weather. It had a waterproof outer section, insulating inner and outer layers of wool pile separated by an air space, a waterproof interior, a vulcanizing seal completely waterproofing and binding inner and outer boot sections, and a felt mid-sole embedded between waterproof inner sole and outer sole. But manufacturers claimed that such a boot could not be produced industrially. Maglio made the first pair by hand and finally persuaded one company to try making them.

But how good were they?

To make doubly sure "they had something," Gianola and Maglio climbed Mount Washington in New Hampshire in the dead of winter to test the boots and cold-weather clothing they had also made. For ten hours, they stayed in a shelter on the mountain with temperatures way below zero. After 15 hours, they got back to civilization.

And the boots? Yes, they stood the test and were soon in use in Korea. And Gianola and Maglio? They were recommended for the Distinguished Civilian Service Award.

Three things move the world:

Ideas, plus
Making them work, plus
Making others like them.

Have We a Worth-while Idea?

Ask yourself two questions. Not only the question, "Can I do it?" But also the question, "Should I?"

The latter is a good test for any undertaking. There are plenty of things in this world that we could do, but, when the job is done, we may have to say, "Well, I guess I wasted my time after all."

It is hardly enough to have just one idea. You should have a number of them, for, smart as you may be, some ideas are not going to pan out. Your constant discovery of ideas must be continuous, for you will have to have supplementary ideas to bolster up the weaknesses you are bound to find in your original conception.

You see, what we are trying to do is to avoid exercising energy on ideas that are not too good in the first place or ideas that have not been carefully worked out and added to and subtracted from and polished until the flaws are no longer there.

One day I was looking out of my hotel window in a southern city and having my thrill of the month. Just across the way, were 30 rookies learning to be firemen. The evening before they had been lowering each other from a six-story building by means of a rope chair and pulley. But this day I was seeing the most thrilling of all sights; they were climbing a building by means of scaling ladders, crossing and recrossing between windows and finally working their way to the top.

I've seen many fires and have never seen scaling ladders used. Have you? Scaling ladders are like long poles, something more than one story in length, with the steps crosswise on the pole and at the end a huge hook that goes right through the window above and hugs the sill. You hook the ladder through the second-story window, and up you go. You carry another ladder with you, and as you reach the second story, you hook that ladder through the third story. Then you may take the other ladder out and carry it to the next story, or with plenty of ladders being handed up, build a complete ladder to the top of the building.

But suppose flames begin to belch out from the window above. You must then cross sidewise to the next line of windows. So you take your spare ladder, reach over, and hook it through the adjoining window above, retaining a grasp on it of course. Next you get your feet on it. You likewise retain a grip on your other ladder, and, when you feel a little secure, pull that ladder out and bring it over so as to have a spare ladder again.

Just when I was getting enthusiastic about these scaling ladders came the letdown. "You know," said a veteran fireman, "in twelve years I've never known these ladders to be used in a fire, and they wouldn't fit any modern building. They were made for the old-style, wide window sills." So I guess the firemen were just having exercise.

It is much like that with many ideas. We often make a great ado over our idea only to find that it does not fit present conditions very well.

In the preceding chapter we referred particularly to people who lack energy. Strangely enough, there are people who have all the energy and "get-up" in the world but not very much of an idea to carry out. They belong in the rhyme!

> *They dash around*
> *Like all get-out,*
> *But when it's over*
> *What was it about?*

These people are steamed up like old-fashioned locomotives standing on a sidetrack. They exert tremendous energy on trivial tasks or, more often, on ideas that have not been well thought out and worked over. While employed in a bank one summer, I was always intrigued by a particular man because he became so enthusiastic over minor tasks that he bumped up and down like a jazz band musician to keep time with the signing of papers, the opening of a letter, or the filing of a note in a pigeonhole. I know another man who almost froths at the mouth with excitement, but his ideas, which start with a great show, almost always collapse.

Are these people what we call "crackpots"? No. "Crackpots" quite often make names in the world, although, generally speaking, I think it better not to be one. Of course, we may be considered queer until we do succeed. In fact, one now successful businessman in a western city seemed no good to his friends and in-laws until some big interests smiled at his invention. Now he has everything, with new plant, new automobile, new home, and new—no, his wife, who once contemplated divorce, has decided to stick it out.

This chapter and the succeeding one should have meaning not only to such individuals but also the great number of people who are *almost* successful with their ideas. The latter let their ideas go to pieces, often to be picked up by some more astute individual and turned into real money, fame, or benefit to the human race.

Your ideas may be like the beryls of San Diego County, California. They just missed being emeralds by virtue of not having any chromium in them.

"You observed everything but failed to reason," the immortal Sherlock Holmes was made to remark.

Let us see if we can simplify the matter and make our paths more pleasant. Let us ask ourselves three questions about any idea:

1. Will it work?
2. Will people accept it?
3. How shall we put it over? (The answer to this third question we shall save for another chapter.)

Will It Work?

Will it work? The practical nature of what we are trying to do is important. There was the strange inventor who wanted to send bombers over Germany to spray the Nazi fighters with cement and turn them into concrete statues. There was the proposal to blow parachute troops away by means of gigantic fans.

But some strange things have worked successfully. In the first world war, the British did train the sea gulls to follow German U-boats and so reveal their presence. This was accomplished by throwing refuse out of English submarines until the gulls came to look for it from U-boats. An amateur did devise the incendiary leaves, which were bits of celluloid coated with phosphorus and thrown from British airplanes to set buildings afire.

Big ideas that involve intricate machinery or heavy promotional campaigns may be too costly. They work in theory, but they do not work financially. They require someone to take too great a risk.

"The non-professional inventor is quite often unable to view his own ideas objectively," says L. S. Hardland of the National Inventors Council. "To him the end product seems sound and workable, and he finds it hard to understand that the expense of development and production far outweighs the usefulness. Assessing the practicality and the practicability of an idea or invention is not easy."

One man thought he had invented a good machine. It would save the company $3,000 a year. That appeared at first sight to be a tidy sum. But it would cost $50,000 to install the machine. If the company had had to borrow that sum, interest and depreciation would have amounted each year to more than $3,000. Why do it?

Several companies refused to accept for production a new type of lawnmower, perfectly good too, because they would have had to scrap their existing manufacturing equipment.

One of our early tasks is to get rid of the "bugs" in our project. You may remember the story of the G. I. in the Korean prison camp. The Chinese were making a great fuss about germ warfare. To impress the G. I. prisoners, they brought in a bug in a jar. It was supposed to be full of deadly germs. But when the prisoners were marched past to see the terrible bug, one G. I. calmly picked it up and swallowed it. That brought the session to a laughing conclusion.

But most ideas do have "bugs" in them. And the best "poisons" are a little experimentation and trial and maybe a change in the idea.

Other people knew about the sewing machine but Elias Howe knew nothing—to begin with. He sat there watching his wife sewing away, trying to see how a machine could imitate that kind of sewing. But then he asked himself, "Why try to imitate her stitch? Why not a new kind of stitch?" He snapped the point off one of his wife's sewing needles and sharpened the head, thus making a needle with an eye at the point. With this he thrust the thread through two pieces of cloth to make a loop. With another needle he passed a second thread through the loop and gently pulled the two threads to tighten the stitch. A half dozen lock stitches were thus quickly made. But would such stitches hold? Howe was so anxious he scarcely had the courage to find out. But, on trying to pull the pieces of cloth apart, he found that the new kind of stitch held even tighter than the common hand stitch.

Edward J. Noble, who after fourteen years sold his Life Saver candy business for $22,000,000, had trouble with his early candy, just as you will find troubles with whatever you are trying to do. The mints stuck together. And worse than that, the flavor would fade away into the cardboard container, and the candy itself would begin to taste of cardboard. He solved his problem with a foil package.

Lee DeForest, as a boy, felt sure that he had discovered the secret of perpetual motion. It was not until years later that he read physics and understood why his idea would not work.

Henry Ford remarked one time that "all the smart people" were proclaiming years ago that the gasoline engine could never compete with steam. But, after some years of work with steam engines, he decided that they were wrong for his purposes. Steam engines were too heavy, and he got more power from the gasoline engine in proportion to weight.

Dr. L. L. Thurstone, the well-known psychologist, who worked with Thomas Edison as a young man, says that Edison always had extra ideas in reserve. "Well, if that doesn't work, we'll try this," Edison would remark.

One great manufacturer left the "bug" in his product and

thereby won astonishing success. What is now Ivory soap was an accident. It had never been intended to float. Making up a batch of the soap one day, a careless workman left the mixing machine running while he went out to lunch. The longer the machine ran the more air it pumped into the soap.

When that batch of soap got into the hands of consumers they liked it. It floated like a piece of cork. Instead of taking their cakes back to the store and asking for a refund, they bought more. And so a great idea developed.

That thought brings us to the next great question.

Will People Accept It?

Your project will ultimately, if not now, be measured by its value to the world. Others may do much deeper and more intricate thinking or perform more experiments, but if the work does not have meaning somewhere, it will not bring permanent recognition.

Will people accept it? Or, more important, will prospective backers support it? Will manufacturers and dealers handle it? And, most important, will the ultimate consumer like it?

"Going to great lengths to sell a man something he does not want is a clumsy way of trying to get money," remarked Harvey S. Firestone. "I have never really had to sell at all— only to explain the favor I expected to do the prospect. The principle holds true, whether one is selling a tangible thing like a rubber tire, or whether one is selling something intangible, like the future of the company, either in the shape of capital stock or in the shape of credit at the bank."

Plenty of things actually work. Successful production may not be a problem. This is particularly true of those creations such as paintings, stories, decorations, designs, etc.

But the mind of the world is a funny thing. You will find that ideas close to the beaten track are more likely to be accepted than those far off and unrelated. Little things may go over more rapidly than great revolutionary ideas which may have to wait for a long while. Fiction was originally frowned upon. "It is neither fish nor flesh nor red herring," remarked the *Edinburgh Review*. "It has no moral value because it is too entertaining." Even little things may be difficult. I remember that I was a pioneer in using two kinds of wallpaper on the side walls of the dining room in a house I had for rent. Today that is common enough, but at the time my prospective tenant lifted her hands in horror and I had to do it over.

One might have thought that the idea of a self-starter for automobiles would have been popular anywhere. But engineers had worked at the problem in Europe and given it up. What do you suppose was the trouble? It was that they feared Europeans would not take to it. You see, European cars were chauffeur-driven, and what was a chauffeur for but to do such things as crank the car?

It was a different story in America. Not only did most owners drive their cars, but friend wife was rapidly coming into the picture as the front- as well as the back-seat driver. So Charles F. Kettering was on a successful track when he built his first electric starter in 1911.

Rudolf Flesch, in his popular book *The Art of Readable Writing*, gets excited over the work of Nebraska University's

Dean L. A. Sherman whose *Analytics of Literature* Flesch terms "one of the most original literary studies ever written." Sherman knew why each word had its particular effect on the reader. He would have delighted the modern business-man because he was unwittingly laying some foundations of modern business and advertising English. But Flesch feels that one of Sherman's important discoveries was the "decrease of predication." Briefly, Sherman called attention to the significant fact that paragraphs and sentences over the years were getting shorter and shorter.

I was taking courses under Dr. Sherman and also under a young rhetoric teacher, Philo Melvin Buck, who later was to become exceedingly popular at the University of Wisconsin. But, as a boy fresh in college, I was greatly impressed by Dean Sherman's class. So in the next English theme for Professor Buck, I chopped mightily. Whole pages became paragraphs, paragraphs became sentences, and sentences mere words. I had become a literary modernist of the twenty-first century.

Professor Buck, reading away in his musty cubbyhole in University Hall, was astonished. "Just what are you doing here!" he exclaimed. "You've spoiled everything."

"Well, you know Dean Sherman's study shows that this is the modern way to do things. Paragraphs and sentences are growing shorter and shorter."

"Now, now!" admonished Professor Buck. "I'm sure Dean Sherman didn't mean to have you apply it like this."

Dean Sherman and the future Dean Buck were both right, but there had to be some middle ground. You always have to do some compromising with the potential public.

Testing Ideas and Products

Nearly all products and ideas have to be tested for workability or salability. But salability, or whether or not people are willing to accept the product, is usually the main point for testing.

How are we going to do this testing? On whom shall we test our idea or product? Friends and relatives? No, I think not. Some relatives and friends will think it wonderful because *you* did it. Other relatives and friends will think it is no good because *you* did it.

In 1805 Sir Walter Scott submitted seven chapters of *Waverley* to a friend for criticism. "Throw them away," the friend advised. "You can't write fiction." Scott took this faulty advice and did lay them away. But, eight years later, he decided to finish the novel for the fun of it. His literary career became a gold mine.

Friends are often simply polite. They are like people in the Orient or other parts of the world. They give you the answer they think you would like to have. A friend of mine in a foreign country asked if there was a bus to the next town. "Oh, yes," was the answer. So he sat down and waited for it. But no bus came. Then he ascertained that actually there was no bus. He asked the man why he had been misdirected. "Oh, I thought you would like to have a bus," the man replied.

Friends and relatives are not objective in opinions. They are usually influenced by their emotions about you. Many times these friends are not helpful. I remember a talk with a boy about a job. He belonged to a wealthy fraternity with plenty of rich fraternity brothers, some in his favored line of work. I suggested that it might be comparatively simple if he got a job with one of them. "Oh, no!" he exclaimed, "they know me *too* well." There was nothing wrong with the boy, but he was encountering the difficulty that so many people encounter when it comes to dealing with friends and relatives. They may think about everything else save the matter itself.

Even experts may be wrong when it comes to appraising the future of your idea. The matter of obtaining an accurate appraisal without a trial is difficult. A successful advertising man questioned whether or not a certain product of mine could be profitably sold by advertising but agreed that the only test would be actual advertising. The results were beyond our most optimistic thought—every time we spent a dollar we got seven or eight dollars in the mail box.

Alex Osborn, famous advertising man, told me one day that an executive must be careful not to discourage an idea or let other people do so when it first comes up. After he has carved the roast beef at one of his employee dinners and the idea forum is opened up, he receives all kinds of ideas. "There are always some people who immediately want to discourage an idea and who begin to think up all the reasons why it will not work," he told me. "But I discourage the criticism, and we put down everything. You never know about ideas at first thought."

The probabilities of a thing succeeding may be small, but the possibilities are always great. So much of this testing is going to devolve upon you, the creator. You'll just have to dig out lots of the answers yourself. But if you are in the field of originating ideas for industry, here is a check list prepared by the U. S. Navy that may help you size up your own idea:

1. *Will it increase production—improve quality?*
2. *Is it a more efficient utilization of man power?*
3. *Does it improve the methods of operation, maintenance, and construction?*
4. *Is it an improvement over the present tools and machinery?*
5. *Does it improve safety?*
6. *Does it prevent waste—conserve materials?*
7. *Does it eliminate unnecessary work?*
8. *Does it reduce costs?*
9. *Does it improve present office methods and procedures?*
10. *Will it improve working conditions?*

"If the answer to any of the above questions is yes," says the Navy, "then you've got a constructive idea!"

John Tigrett, toy manufacturer of Jackson, Tennessee, tests his prospective toys on not unwilling school children. Children have minds the same as adults, and what one thinks they will surely enjoy can turn out to be the thing that will have to wait eternally on the dealer's shelf. So he persuades one of the new-fangled schoolma'ms to let him put on a gadget show. He mixes his doodads in with those of other manufacturers and lets the children have a grand hour with them. Then he gives each child a quarter, and the child buys the toy he would like to have. If the children select all the toys of his competitors instead of his own, he knows his ideas are not "hot" ones. But if, as often happens, half of the children want the toy he is considering making, he feels sure that success is on the way.

The reason for so much preliminary testing is to avoid a $10,000 loss by spending maybe $100. We do not want to be like Mark Twain who got started on a typesetting machine and kept piling in more and more money until he had spent a fortune.

To make the test cheaply is important. To do the preparatory work cheaply is equally important. Even the government sees this problem in its wartime work. It costs only 22 cents an hour to operate a typical bomber simulator in which crews for big bombers are trained as compared with $242 an hour for operating a real bomber. And the initial cost of a flight simulator is only one-eighth that of the real thing.

Large newspapers will permit advertisers to test two pieces of advertising on payment of a small premium. One-half of all the papers will contain one advertisement and the other half another advertisement, both dealing with the same product. It does not take long that way to determine which is the better piece of advertising if the advertisement carries an offer designed to bring direct response from readers.

Maybe the entire idea can be worked out on a low-cost basis. What a blessing when that can be done!

The early idea of *Time* magazine turned what many people would have considered a liability into an asset. Generally it takes enormous money to put a magazine across. But *Time* was to be a little magazine that did not waste your time. Everything was to be summarized for a few minutes reading. Here was just the thing for a busy man or woman. What a wonderful idea that was for Publisher Henry Luce! His sales idea was the very thing that kept his expenses to a minimum. He did not have to spend thousands of dollars on a pretentious publication, trusting that finally subscribers and advertising would come in. He made a little money go a long way. Of course today *Time* never mentions that original idea, for advertising volume is large and the magazine no longer small.

One of the great electrical companies makes constant "value studies" of its products, even after they are out on the market. One machine has a switch that costs $100, but there are electric switches that cost 15 cents. Both turn electricity on and off. What's the difference? Is too much money being spent on that other machine? Would a cheaper job do the work every bit as well?

The prospective dealer is often "a hard nut to crack." He has had so many failures that often he cannot see a real success. But without revealing too many of the details of your idea, you may ask prospective dealers or users how they would react to it. If possible, make up a few samples and try them out, just to get the reaction of shopkeepers. I know one young man who could have saved himself a great deal of effort by peddling his product to a few stores before getting in too deep. He had a perfectly good silver cleaner, but there was not enough consumption of the item to warrant stores' stocking much of it. Another company had a product with somewhat similar composition. But they were using it for a paint remover with silver cleaning as a sideline. They had enlarged its possibilities.

Occasionally, publishing houses advertise books before they accept them for publication, just to see if orders come in. One man actually advertised his book—a mail order one—

before he wrote it. Orders piled in, and then he had to sit up nights for a month to write it.

Every man, every business has to do a bit of this testing, whether it be the product itself or only a circular. You have no doubt often marvelled about those ingenious letters that you receive from *Time* magazine, letters that fairly make you want to get out your pen and sign on the dotted line. You might think that *Time* knows all about the letter-writing business. Well, it admits that it doesn't know everything because, before it starts out on a circular letter campaign, it has half a dozen letters ready, any one of which should delight the heart of a sales manager. But it is a serious matter, when you are sending out hundreds of thousands of circulars and they are not pulling as they should, to think that maybe you made a mistake and should have used another approach.

Well, what does *Time* do? It tries out its good letters all at the same time in limited quantities. After a few weeks, it becomes apparent which letter is pulling the best. *Time* often lets college students prejudge the sample letters and then awards free subscriptions to those who can list the letters in the correct order of their actual drawing power. But this does not cost *Time* very many free subscriptions for comparatively few prejudge them correctly.

One year almost no one in the entire country did so, and *Time* gave the subscriptions to those who came close. I recall a boy "who came close." Strangely, he had had no training in advertising, publicity, or writing. He came from a farm. But it was obvious why his judgment was good. He had not stopped to think about theories, experiences of advertisers, and rules out of textbooks. He had simply looked at it all as a man would out in a small town and asked himself, "Which one of these letters would make *me* send in *my* money?" He came close and so did not have to send in any money at all—he got a free subscription.

Another young man was examining a vast amount of circular material which I had distributed one day. He was doing the advertising and promotional work for an appliance company. Suddenly he picked up one piece out of the heap. "Isn't this awful!" he exclaimed, holding it up to ridicule. But, on second thought, he remarked, "If you don't mind, I'm going to keep this circular and order that thing."

So play with your idea. Test it. Prove it. Do this occasionally as you develop the idea. Do not forget the two tests: Will it work? Will people accept it? The final and great test of course is actually selling the idea to the world, but that we leave to succeeding chapters.

How to Put It Over

I ARRIVED THIS AFTERNOON at four o'clock, on the steamboat, from Albany. As the success of my experiment gives me great hope that such boats may be rendered of much importance to my country, to prevent erroneous opinions, and give some satisfaction to the friends of useful improvements, you will have the goodness to publish the following statement of fact."

That was Robert Fulton, acting as his own press agent, in spreading abroad the fact that he had made a successful trip in his steamboat. You might have thought that newspapers would have recounted with breathless interest every movement of his boat, but Robert Fulton was almost completely ignored, and he had to write an account of the trip and send it to the newspaper, which promptly hid it away on an inside page.

You are now in the same class with Robert Fulton and George Stephenson and the Wright Brothers. That is, you have something to put over, and the world may not be too anxious to see what you have.

One of George Stephenson's great accomplishments was not in developing the locomotive but *in selling a company on the idea of using it* instead of a horse on a tramway.

After they had made their historic flight in 1903, the Wright Brothers asked the government if it would be interested in experiments with a flying machine. It replied that it was definitely not interested in "financing experiments," and *several years passed* before the government agreed to buy a machine.

Sitting in your plush seat in a moving picture theater, you accept talking pictures as a matter of course. It is hard to think of them otherwise. You and I forget that talking pictures arrived in the lifetime of most of us. I recall attending the first series of such productions in New York one summer. There was excellent attendance at premium prices—people liked them.

One might have thought the original idea a "push-over," particularly with the backing of the great Bell Telephone System. Bell Telephone had created a billion-dollar idea, but, like an aspiring movie actor, it beat vainly on the doors of Hollywood. Finally a telephone man from the west coast saw a demonstration in New York and prevailed upon Sam Warner to see it, too. Sam Warner saw it and believed. Other movie men expected the idea to fail, but it did not. Warner's confounded the moving picture world by succeeding. The people liked the idea, but the middlemen had not anticipated that fact.

[203]

I start with these notes of caution not to discourage but to encourage developers of ideas with the thought that successful men of the world had their problems, too.

But these men learned to vanquish their obstacles.

Do Something about It

I early learned that the defect of so many students, and grownups too, with Phi Beta Kappa minds is their inability to cope with reality. They are scared when it comes to going out and practicing their learning, particularly when it involves convincing someone else that the product of their learning is really good after all. Also few students have "talking points" or "experience points" to use in their own interest when it comes to position hunting. They have never enjoyed the thrill of success in a hard undertaking. Prospective employers love people who can do something about matters.

Thousands of good, if not great, things never came into existence or withered on the vine because they did not receive the attention of the world or the world did not accept them. Three hundred years ago, we were almost on the verge of discovering artificial silk. What a different development the world might have had if artificial silk had come into existence! Or what might have happened had oil and the gasoline engine antedated steam and people had thought in terms of highways rather than railroads?

I had been called to attend a meeting of some executives of a great corporation to help discuss this matter of creativity. Most of the men were from the engineering and production branches and were right in their element—invention.

"But don't forget us," a heavy-set executive from the head office remarked. "We've got to market the product, and we need ideas, too." In putting your own idea across, you are going to find that still more ideas are needed. Often they may be, and many times must be, better than the original one.

If you are in business for yourself or likely to get into business, or engaged in any of the arts, or just seeking to do good in the world, you have an excellent opportunity to use your ideas right at home.

Your idea might finally be a business in itself.

Here, for instance, is a university girl who was dead set on a radio program. Did she go down and badger the proprietor of one of the local stations for a part-time job? Did she take courses and more courses telling her "how to do it?" Quite the contrary. She conceived her own idea of a little radio program, went down and secured a sponsor (a local theater), and then walked into the radio station, not to seek a beginner's job but actually to buy time for her own production. She made enough to keep her in school and had a good time doing it. Best of all, after graduation she never had the slightest difficulty in securing good positions, for she was no longer a beginner without experience. She had been through the mill herself and had met the problems of a small business.

But what kind of an idea have you? Ask yourself what it is that you are trying to accomplish. It is strange indeed that so many people are not quite sure of their ultimate aim. They expect to shoot into the sky and bring down a duck, a pigeon, or maybe a captive balloon.

For some people their ideas are important inventions; for

[205]

others their ideas are doodads for the dime store. For some their ideas are great books or works of art; for others their idea is to get a little more money into the family pocketbook. For some their ideas are magnificent ones of doing tremendous good in the world, the kind of ideas that would delight the heart of the *Reader's Digest*. For others their ideas are only to keep school children happy and ambitious.

Ideas run all the way from a paper clip to a hydrogen bomb.

What shall you do to make your idea a reality?

Try publicity, the first person says.

Try salesmanship, the second advises.

Try advertising, recommends the third.

Naturally the more you learn to use "these tricks of the trade," the better off you will be. And, if you have time, I recommend that you read some books dealing with those subjects.

But, basically, before we consider details, you must remember that your task is to get your idea before the world, or your selected part of the world, and make people like it.

The world is a great sea of things and ideas. Some of them stay up, and some sink. But you have got to make yours stand above the others.

In the beginning the world may be indifferent. It may even dislike you and your idea.

It is *emphasis* that turns the trick! *Emphasis* and more *emphasis* and still more *emphasis!* Whether it be publicity or salesmanship or advertising, it is this steady hammering at people with basic ideas that finally wins out. This may take considerable time.

If you have ever had to deal with people in foreign countries, you will often find that you have to explain your idea and keep repeating it until finally it occurs to them what you mean and what you want. That principle accounts for the long speeches of Russian representatives always working on the same themes.

Years ago, when the world was more peaceful I myself tried the same technique in Moscow—on the Russians. Like most tourists, I found myself assigned to the National Hotel. Outside tourists still generally stay at the National. But up the street was the great Moskva Hotel, the Waldorf-Astoria of the city, then virtually completed. I thought how nice it would be to stay there. My advance payment was not in line with the fantastic prices they asked for accommodations, and it was usually full to the rafters. But I decided to explore the situation. So I called on them, not once, not twice, but three times. Each time I would explain that the old National Hotel was far below the standards of first-class American hotels and that certainly the Russians would not want Americans to go home with recollections of having stayed there.

Finally they succumbed and resignedly remarked, "Bring your things over here." I was escorted down the corridor to a great front room, with five windows, two tables, a desk, and modernistic furniture strewn about in great profusion, all at the same price I was paying up the street.

Basically, it is this same principle that works for all of us individually—making the other fellow do what we would like to have him do, and, if at first he is indifferent or doesn't want to, getting him to change his mind. "All specialists face the problem of convincing," says E. L. Bernays, famous consultant in public relations. "The specialist cannot control the layman; he must convince and persuade him."

A publisher was walking through his stockroom one day— so the story goes—and saw great stacks of unsold books neatly hidden away on the back shelves. "What's that book?" he asked.

"Oh, a lady's written a book on etiquette," he was jokingly told.

He decided to try to turn those books into money with original advertising ideas, and Emily Post, etiquette authority, was born. It is reasonable to suppose that Emily Post would have remained unknown to the multitudes without special work in her behalf.

Ministers got behind *The Magnificent Obsession,* gave Lloyd Douglas real momentum, and the great vogue for religious novels was born, or rather revived.

Almost anything can be put across if enough money is spent in advertising and promotion. But, unfortunately, that does not mean that it will prove a profitable undertaking. The cost of selling your doodad might be two dollars. But if you were getting only one dollar for the article, you would be like the man who boasted before he went into bankruptcy, "The reason I can sell below cost is because I sell so much." Anyone can dump goods at great price concessions, but that does not help out in the profit column.

So one of the great purposes of creating ideas is to avoid having to sell at so low a price that the profit disappears. Some old stores have developed such famous names that they remove themselves from price-cutting competition. But newer companies have to have ideas.

Putting that something extra into your product that makes

it no longer necessary to sell on a price-competitive basis is the desire of hundreds of companies and individuals. One of the splendid examples of handling a problem of this sort is Dr. West's toothbrush. Older readers will remember when you walked into a store, felt the bristles on half a dozen toothbrushes and bought the one you liked. But it really was a simple idea to package each brush separately and emphasize the sanitary quality of the brush. Of course, such a procedure was supplemented by a constant series of new developments that took the product out of the ordinary, such as waterproof and nylon bristles and transparent tubes for the product.

But let us for a moment step back to that idea of sanitary containers for a product. How many things can you think of offhand that might be improved and made more salable in that way? Maybe your product needs dressing up with that idea.

Suppose you exercise your mind a bit and carry that idea of attractive and sanitary handling further, carry it far back of the retailer or wholesaler. I can remember a college class with a number of agricultural students and also a number of women from the first families of the city. One of the students unwittingly revealed the refuse that many hogs eat. A woman immediately threw up her hands in horror. "I never want to eat another bit of pork!" she exclaimed.

You are a gentleman farmer and you begin to think of the "contented cows" of Carnation Milk. So why not pork products from your farm where the filthy hog lot exists no longer and animals receive only selected feeds? There are probably tens of thousands of families in the United States who would be willing to pay a handsome premium for pork products from such farms. And immediately you are back to the principle of Dr. West's toothbrush—a more desirable sanitary product for which a better price might be obtained.

J. Wray Taylor, living near Denver, developed a butter and egg business despite high prices because he turned out a quality product and sold it to wealthy families in the mountain and foothill districts. He found that his dressed poultry easily brought more than double the price he would have obtained had he sold it on the ordinary market.

Collins & Aikman had a problem in promoting the use of its Candalon upholstery for motor cars. Automobile manufacturers had always emphasized outside appearance, color, and performance. Not much had been said about interiors. Besides too many dealers were anxious to sell a set of seat covers with a car and so never mentioned upholstery. But Collins & Aikman had an idea. Why not emphasize upholstery and point out that the Candalon seats were so good that no seat covers would be needed? That was an interesting selling argument for auto dealers and enabled them to steal an automobile sale from competitors even if they were not able to sell a set of seat covers.

No one knows just how much sales resistance the world will offer to your product. And it is hard to determine without a test. You will see in many magazines and newspaper supplements, such as *The New York Times Magazine*, hundreds of small advertisements that offer things to eat, things to wear, things for pure ornament—most of them advertisements of small companies trying to sell directly to the consumer. If your product is of that character, examine many publications that feature this type of advertising and give your product a try. I have seen the expenditure of $15 to

$50 dollars, sometimes less, in advertising show that articles did have surprising appeal to the public. If success greets you, you may enlarge the scope of your advertising.

Or you may try direct mail, selecting for your letter and circular a few thousand concerns or people that should be interested. Lists of people interested in certain lines are usually obtained from mailing list houses that charge about $15 a thousand for use of names. That is why you may receive so many circular letters—your name is on these lists.

But I hope you will not be as successful as Beta, an English company that set out to tap the United States market for cashmere sweaters. Preliminary study showed that they might be able to sell 500 sweaters as a result of an advertisement they were preparing for a New York newspaper. But astonishment turned to dismay when the orders shot far beyond 6,000 and there were simply not enough sweaters to go around nor could any more be obtained within a reasonable time. So money just had to be returned with regrets.

Years ago, the Bradley Knitting Company had a very different experience. It started to merchandise bathing suits in the Middle West. The people liked bathing suits, but the dealers confided to the company that the people had no place to swim. So the company had to start on the herculean task of getting a swimming pool into every town. And not a little of the popularity of the swimming pool was due to that company's early activity.

This was somewhat akin to the experience of the Mutual Security Administration in getting farmers to grow corn in France. They raised the corn readily enough and then came the question, "How do you harvest it?" Mechanical corn pickers were out of the question on most farms. So they sent for expert corn-grower Elmer Carlson of Audubon, Iowa. He introduced the American husking hook and by dint of practical demonstration taught the French easy and rapid corn-husking.

Manufacturers, for example, often spend a great deal of time worrying over their product's being in the current popular trend. Many books have established trends—believed not to exist—and publishers have come along in their wake. But one has to figure promotion costs carefully. Astonishing as it may seem, the advertising cost of Dale Carnegie's book, *How to Win Friends and Influence People,* was for a considerable time $1.42 for each $1.96 book sold, as far as the direct replies from advertising were concerned. That would have created an impossible situation had it not been for the additional copies sold through bookstores as a general result of the advertising.

Obviously the things that are easiest to put across are those that do not have too high a production or promotion cost. That little margin in between is what makes a concern a great success rather than a bankrupt house. It may be very slight.

Here is an important suggestion. It is often just the extra idea that puts the thing across, the last punch in the merchandising or the construction of the advertisement. I have watched with breathless interest while Frank Egner, a mail order authority, changed a word here or a word there in a bit of promotional material to make it sell just a little more. Or perhaps the product itself is changed so that it works a little better or is a little more attractive. Maybe your project will not be a failure after all. We were talking about this extra quality after seeing a new musical comedy in Tokyo. It was just "so-so," but two great melodies would have supplied what was lacking.

You may do as Robert Fulton did—carry out some publicity on your own behalf. Many magazines, particularly trade or specialized magazines, devote attention to new developments and inventions in their fields. You will find comprehensive lists of such magazines in the back pages of Ayer's *Directory of Newspapers and Periodicals,* specializing in everything from air conditioning to rabbit raising. This book is to be found in the reference rooms of nearly all city libraries.

After locating the name and address of the magazine, you turn to the city in the front part of the directory and learn further details, including the name of the editor. Then you may prepare or have prepared a suitable announcement and possibly photographs of your innovation and send it to the editor, trusting that he will give it some notice. If your work is of a "world-shaking" character, he might even give you a big feature story. Occasionally even famous magazines, such as *Life,* devote attention to such matters. Carrying on publicity work is something like prospecting. You never know for sure just where the favorable attention will break forth. I have actually had the press associations carry indirect publicity material to all corners of the country and Canada with great success and yet, at the time, the manager of the press bureau was not quite sure that papers would like it. The more you look about, the more opportunities you will see for such promotion. Scores of magazines devote paragraphs to new developments. Look for those publications.

Publicity may not produce sales as rapidly as paid advertising for the simple reason that it becomes background material. It does not sell directly but arouses interest.

Those Medium-sized Ideas

So many ideas are "betwixt and between" ideas. They are not inventions or books or paintings. They are just smaller ideas that we would like to follow in our everyday lives. Sometimes these ideas are nothing more than the solution of little problems. But they are very important to people in everyday living or business.

So I have, for a good many years, conducted a course where the outside work consists in the student's "putting something over." Each student has his own project and, during the semester, seeks to bring it to a successful conclusion. It is not always a successful conclusion either. Quite often it is unsuccessful, but the student, in the process, learns why a venture succeeds and why it fails. And how often it is just the little extra idea that turns the trick!

A young man found that he could be a successful travel agent. He undertook the somewhat difficult task of organizing a skiing tour for the students of a corn-belt university. Whoever would have thought that students in the flat lands would favor such a project? He had to sell many of them on skiing and then on the trip. He plastered doors in university buildings with preliminary notices, published stories in the campus newspaper, pep-talked people into its possibilities. And when Christmas vacation came, off went a considerable delegation 700 miles to the mountains. Publicity, propaganda, advertising, and salesmanship are great things in putting an idea over. But he found that the most important problem was to sustain interest from the time of the initial meeting right up to the day of the trip. In other words, *keep* the potential customers enthusiastic.

A strange situation developed in an honorary sorority, one of those scholastic organizations that elect so many bright girls on the basis of scholarship in certain fields each year. One year, they elected the girls, but neglected the important matter of securing the initiation payment. The question of what to do about it arose several years later. Clearly those fees should have been paid, but no one had thought much about it. And now the sorority needed that money. What do you do in such a case? What kind of approach do you make? Do you just send them a bill? Not exactly, in a case like this —a bill could be postponed or laid aside. And you don't excommunicate your sorority sister, so to speak.

The most successful solution was the simplest idea, as often happens. Each of the young women received a letter, the kind of letter each would like to receive and yet one that could not be completely disregarded. In no sense was it a dunning letter. It was a very personal letter from one of the girls in the active chapter, written in longhand. The letter started out telling of pleasant things—how the grand old school was getting on and what the university department was doing, what the teachers and girls looked like these days, and such matters. Then finally, toward the close of the letter, came the reminder that some of the members had never paid the initiation fee and that the individual addressed was one of them. The sorority needed the money and how delighted it would be to receive it! Everyone was surprised when the money rolled in—a very substantial sum indeed. The idea as to the proper approach had been a brilliant one.

In a depression year, one student took for his project that of securing a position at graduation. Comfortable salaries were hard to secure that year. So he undertook the herculean task of sending 500 letters to some 500 quite important corporations. He thus acquired an advantage over other students in that he accumulated experience in many side projects that he carried on successfully during his college course. He acquired talking points in his behalf, just as other students were at the moment acquiring side experience through individual projects.

This young man got results. Corporations sent representatives to interview him. There was one position for which he had been angling a considerable time. But the man back of it was not sure that "a boy just out of school" would do. When he showed some of the letters he was getting from other prospective employers, the company closed the deal with him at once.

One of the boys, who confidentially told me that he had been making $3,500 a year while attending school, was doing publicity for a night club. But one Friday night, the University itself competed with its own event, one that most of the students wanted to attend. What do you do in a case like that? He had to turn oncoming defeat for the night club into success. He did it by a little advertising coupon on the program of the University's event offering a special price to students attending the night club after the University's event was over. It worked, and he got the crowd after all.

A problem confronted a young man engaged in selling advertising space in an unusual farm publication. Not counting the time that it took to sell the space itself, he found that often several trips were necessary before he could secure the elusive copy from a particular merchant. So he stuffed his head with copy ideas beforehand, and the minute he had the storekeeper saying, "Yes," he would say, "Let's do it right now." He and the merchant would sit down and turn out the advertisement on the spot.

Simple ideas to help out other ideas? Yes, but they work.

$\big\{$16

Selling and Protecting Your Ideas

It is a long time from the early days of Chris Steenstrup. Chris Steenstrup one day nearly lost his job with General Electric when he suggested a brilliant idea. But he lived to tell the tale and later became one of the great engineers of the corporation. Chris had invented a much faster and safer method of feeding sheet metal to the presses. But, when he suggested the plan to his foreman, Chris found himself discharged because he was not supposed to think about such things. Fortunately, in the nick of time, the incident came to the attention of the plant manager, who ordered the idea adopted.

In this day of personnel departments and better educated foremen, it is extremely doubtful if such an incident could occur in a large company. A corporation that doesn't stay alert enough to study every money-making idea doesn't deserve to stay in business very long, and usually doesn't.

There are tens of thousands of ideas produced every day in the United States, for in the final analysis nearly everyone produces some ideas, good, bad and indifferent, but often without realizing that he is producing ideas.

Every company and every institution has to have ideas and will have to have more ideas in the future. A company is an abstract something, and that means that some human being has to supply the ideas. Machines do not supply ideas, but people do. There is one everlasting victory that man has over the machine. Machines simply do what they are told to do.

How to get ideas and users together is the problem. Obviously one of the possible users of ideas is your own company; that is, if the idea is one that will fit that company. And virtually all corporations today have set up comprehensive schemes, known as suggestion systems, for dealing with employee's ideas and paying for them. Few men today will have the experience of Chris Steenstrup.

"If all our production and scientific experts had the mental assistance and cooperation of the total artisan group, in an orderly process, the production achievements of our combined efforts would be beyond our greatest expectations," says F. E. Raterman, executive secretary of the Navy Efficiency Awards Committee. "The consequent increase in the supply of available goods at a cost which would make a reasonable distribution possible would be the answer to one phase of our goal for industrial peace.

"The next phase, which, in the total picture is perhaps of even greater importance than the first, is the satisfaction of the human desires of the individual. Some call them emotional or spiritual desires, but I am sure that all realize that I speak of those needs beyond the material. . . . What we need is an appeal to the self-satisfaction of the individual by encouraging his mental efforts along with his physical endeavors. If each employee in industry, commerce, and government could be made to feel that he had a share in the problems of management, and that he also had some responsibility for assisting in their solution, we could not help but produce a feeling of confidence and cooperation."

A company may have laboratories and skilled engineers, but often those individuals fail to see great possibilities. But along comes Jim Smith or Sally Jones with a valuable idea. "The man close to the job is often in the best position to find a better way, despite competent methods men, research engineers, and alert supervisors," remarks G. A. Price, president of Westinghouse. Westinghouse Electric thinks so much of employee suggestions that it has doubled its awards based on the annual savings resulting from these ideas.

What you will receive as a monetary award depends a great deal on the nature of the company and the magnitude of its operations. A small company might not make as large annual savings as another whose products are universally used. But its operations may be of such character that it can pay proportionately more for its ideas.

Bell & Howell awards successful suggestion creators with cash amounts that are based on 50 per cent of the net saving for the first year of use, or 10 per cent of the gross saving when a heavy capital investment is involved. Recently a woman noted that time was wasted mimeographing descriptions of small parts on paper slips and pasting them to envelopes. Why not stamp the specifications on the envelopes in the first place? She received $3,425 for her idea. Often, when problems arise, employees are called in for suggestions.

A foreman in Swift & Company received $5,600 for his pork-cutting machine. A Pullman porter was given $750 for an idea that saved the company woolen goods and cleaning bills. *The Wall Street Journal* believes that the highest award ever paid by a suggestion system was $28,800 given by the Clevite Corporation to a foundry worker who thought up a new process for making graphite bearings.

One of the most indefatigable workers in the field of employee suggestion systems is F. A. Denz of Remington Rand. He keeps right after employees and supervisors for more and more ideas. Here is the Remington Rand method for people to get their ideas across in that organization:

"INTRODUCE: Show need. Showing is more effective than telling.

"PRESENT: Organize. Sketch. Picture. Diagram. Model. Condense but explain each point.

"SUMMARIZE: State briefly result and advantages. Restress need."

"Don't give up readily" is the advice in that organization. "You've got to plan an idea. You've got to be creative in planning."

Protecting Your Idea

But suppose you don't work for a company that uses the kind of idea you happen to have. You may have decided that you do not want to handle it yourself. Or, at least, you want to explore the possibilities of selling out to someone else. Almost the first thing you think of is how to protect your idea.

So you want your rights, do you? This is a universal problem among those who create ideas—how do you prevent someone else from running off with that precious idea of *yours*? And here you enter upon a subject that is the delight of the legal profession, for thousands of suits have for their beginnings an infringement of an idea.

The situation reminds me of the day the president of a company was interviewing a man for head of a department. "How much authority will I have?" asked the man.

"Well, I think you will have just about as much as you can get," answered the president. And it is something like that in protecting your idea or invention. You have about as many rights as you can get and keep.

What protection do you have against someone's appropriating your idea, either stealing it outright or accidentally creating the same thing after you have already made it? Libraries and bookstores are full of volumes that deal at great length with patents and copyrights, and I recommend that you browse through as many such books as you like in order to obtain an accurate knowledge of the protection of your creations and court decisions bearing thereon.

In the first place, of course, you must ask yourself whether or not you want or need protection on your idea. There are thousands of ideas put into circulation for which the originators desire no protection and other thousands of rather abstract ideas for which probably no protection could be obtained.

Many people engaged in "doing good" are only too happy

to see their ideas used. Government departments, colleges and their extension services, churches, city health departments and public school systems exist for the purpose of benefiting the world.

There are likewise hundreds of ideas that people create from day to day and use but once. Most of the ideas used by students in the examples in the preceding chapter were good ones, but a person would not desire to protect them even if he could. Any business executive from week to week creates dozens of ideas, valuable but not patentable. That, incidentally, is why executives receive large salaries.

Likewise, an investor may discover a valuable bond of a bankrupt corporation and start buying up the bonds. But he just keeps quiet until he has bought up as many as he desires. Then he usually doesn't care how many other people begin buying, for the more they buy the higher the price they pay. And he makes money on the increase in value.

Now we come to a significant matter. All courts lean to the rule that any idea protected by law must be reduced to concrete form. The government and courts cannot offer protection to some abstraction. For instance, one could not patent or copyright the Christian religion. But when certain parts of it are reduced to concrete form, protection may be given. Strangely enough, many Bibles have been copyrighted, as you will find by examining their front pages. This is usually to afford the translators and scholars a monetary return for the particular job.

The action of the investor in buying the bonds of the defunct corporation is not something that he can restrict to himself. But an investment service suggesting that investors buy up such bonds may copyright its bulletins and sell them.

[223]

The Bible and the bulletin reduce the protection to concrete form although the copyright on them does not prevent anyone reading either of them from utilizing the information.

A patent, which generally covers mechanical invention, and is procurable from the United States Patent Office in Washington, D.C., gives you 17 years of exclusive right to your invention. I would recommend that, if your interest lies in procuring a patent, you first of all write to the Patent Office and ask for the circular entitled, *General Information concerning Patents.* Then, after you have gone through it, you will have an excellent idea of the possibilities and limitations of patents.

Patents have a long and eventful history in the United States dating clear back to the provision in the Constitution providing that "Congress shall have the power . . . to promote the progress of science and useful arts, by securing for limited times to authors and inventors the exclusive right to their respective writings and discoveries."

As the Patent Office expresses it:

"In the language of the statute any person who 'invents or discovers any new and useful process, machine, manufacture, or composition of matter, or any new and useful improvement thereof, may obtain a patent,' subject to the conditions and requirements of the law. By the word 'process' is meant a process or method, and new processes, primarily industrial or technical processes, may be patented. . . .

"The statute specifies that the subject matter must be 'useful.' The term 'useful' in this connection refers to the condition that the subject matter has a useful purpose and also includes operativeness, that is, a machine which will not operate to perform the intended purpose would not be called useful."

But—

"Interpretations of the statute by the courts have defined the limits of the field of subject matter which can be patented, thus it has been held that methods of doing business and printed matter cannot be patented. In the case of mixtures of ingredients, such as medicines, a patent cannot be granted unless there is more to the mixture than the effect of its components. So-called patent medicines are not patented; the phrase 'patent medicine' in this connection does not have the meaning that the medicine is patented. It is often said that a patent cannot be obtained upon a mere idea or suggestion. The patent is granted upon the new machine, manufacture, etc.,—and not upon the idea or suggestion of the new machine."

Ordinarily a patent costs $30 for the filing fee and $30 for the final fee.

But again—

You might as well disregard the moderate sum you pay the government for this patent, because you will first of all want to hire a patent lawyer. You will want a preliminary search made to see whether or not your proposal conflicts with patents already in existence and if it does whether or not you can get around these conflicts. And, of course, you will have to have accurate drawings and possibly a model of the invention. When your patent is "going through the mill" you may find that some of your claims will be rejected and others sustained. Your lawyer will guide you. All in all, a patent will usually cost anywhere from a few hundred dollars to several thousand dollars before the job is wrapped up and delivered to you.

You may find that your proposed patent infringes on something already patented. A man engaged in getting a household device ready for market for a large corporation told me that they had found, after the job had been done, that it apparently infringed on basic patents another company had taken out. The problem then was for the man to discover new ideas that might enable the company to get around the other patents or possibly to attack the patents of the other company in court.

The startling thing about both patents and copyrights is the fact that you yourself have to enforce them. When someone steals your invention and starts manufacturing it, you have to start the suit to maintain your rights. Likewise, you may be called upon to defend your patent if someone institutes action to break it. The courts become superior to the Patent Office. In other words, you may have to fight for your rights even after you have them.

Securing a copyright is a much simpler undertaking than that of securing a patent. A copyright for a book may be had for four dollars simply by filling out the proper blanks and depositing two completed copies with the Copyright Office, Library of Congress, Washington, D.C. Copyrightable material also includes periodicals; lectures; dramatic and musical compositions; maps; art work, illustrations and photographs; and motion pictures. Some people think they can get around a patent for a mechanical device by taking out a copyright on the plans and descriptions. But that does not prevent anyone from building the device; it simply protects your few pages of description from being reproduced. Many books telling you how to make things are copyrighted, but that does not prevent a person from building the things in question.

Some things that seem patentable come under copyright instead. Mickey Mouse and Elsie the Cow are copyrighted and find their place in many doodads, but it is not the mechanical construction of the doodad that is under protection. Rather it is the Mickey Mouse or Elsie the Cow picture. Without them, the stuffed animal would be unsalable. The copyright takes care of works of a literary or artistic nature. But it does not offer an easy way of securing the exclusive right to an idea, plan, or method.

A copyright runs for 28 years and is renewable for another 28 years. If you are interested in copyrights, write to the Register of Copyrights, Library of Congress, Washington, D.C. for the appropriate blanks and specify the nature of the material you desire to protect.

Trademarks are something else again but are often useful when you want to implant in the public mind some design or mark that associates your company with particular products. It is not a patent or a copyright. In government language, a trademark includes "any word, name, symbol, or device or any combination thereof adopted and used by a manufacturer or merchant to identify his goods and distinguish them from those manufactured or sold by others. . . . The primary function of a trademark is to indicate origin. However, trademarks also serve to guarantee the quality of the goods bearing the mark and, through advertising, serve to create and maintain a demand for the product. Rights in a trademark are acquired only by use and the use must ordinarily continue if the rights so acquired are to be preserved."

You register your trademark in the Patent Office at Washington, and it costs $25 as the basic fee. A trademark is protected for 20 years and may be renewed. May I suggest that if you desire to explore the possibilities of trademarks you write to the United States Patent Office, Washington, D.C., for the bulletin on *General Information concerning Trademarks*.

Is there any other way that a person may hang on to his rights? Courts are inclined to frown on people who steal things and have decided that the creators of ideas do have rights in them and ideas may not be appropriated without recompense when they are submitted to possible purchasers. A beer slogan submitted by an advertising agency was held to be worth $7,500 when the agency failed to get the account but the slogan was used by the brewing company. A large cigaret manufacturer was assessed $9,000 because it appeared to the jury that the basic idea of a famous advertisement was similar to that previously submitted by the plaintiff.

May I make a suggestion here that you keep a record of the dates you conceive your idea and the dates on which you take steps toward its fulfillment? You may, if you desire, send yourself a registered letter with the information contained therein, and keep the letter unopened. This procedure does not take the place of a patent or copyright; it simply establishes your position in the matter when someone else might be applying for a patent at the same time you are doing so. Or it might be valuable court evidence in case someone gets hold of your piece of work.

[228]

But now you are ready to sell your invention or other piece of work to someone else who supposedly is going to pay you a good royalty for a long time. Your problem is the critical problem of selling anything—finding the company or firm that is interested in buying it.

And how are you going to find that company? The knowledge that a patent has been granted in a certain field becomes public knowledge to most firms concerned. There is also a patent register at the United States Patent Office where you may record a notice of your invention for all to see.

But this probably will not be enough. Like the seller of anything, you have to find and, more often, convince the potential individual or company that you have something worth while. This often means a personal approach, usually by letter. And whom shall you approach?

First it may pay you to go to your public library and, in the reference department, ask to be shown the directories of manufacturers in different fields. If you are interested in toys, find the toy manufacturers; if in boots and shoes, the shoe manufacturers; and so on. There they all are. In addition to directories of manufacturers, you will find directories of directories, in other words, books that tell you where you may find highly specialized compilations of the names of manufacturers in certain lines.

Your first letter may well call attention to what you have, its good points and its possibilities. Then, if the company is interested, it will ask you for more information. See that your letter is well typed and gives the impression that you are a successful and responsible individual. You may have to do a lot of this before you strike pay dirt.

[229]

You might advertise your invention in financial newspapers, or you might use paid advertising in the trade papers. Again, you might send publicity material to trade papers as we suggested in the preceding chapter in discussing the promotion of ideas.

Basically, you go through the same process in selling the rights to anything—ideas, books, art. You have to locate the people interested.

But now we come to a highly significant point. It is often not so much the idea or invention that is valuable by itself as the promotion that has gone into building it up. Millions of dollars were paid, it is true, for the Life Saver candy business and the Toni home permanents. But in the beginning those ideas were worth little. It was the build-up that made them valuable. The original Coca Cola recipe brought less than a few shares of the stock would today. But Coca Cola was made valuable by advertising and promotion.

So, if you are not going to engage in the actual manufacture or promotion of your invention, idea, or product, you have two possibilities open to you: sell it to your employer or, when it has little connection with your employer's business or your own business, sell it to outside interests. And you may find it advisable to take steps to protect your idea. Secure the circulars mentioned in this chapter from the government. Then, if things seem complicated, read some books dealing with patent and copyright protection found in any bookstore or library. Do not be dismayed if you have to spend a great deal of time at promotion and protection; profitable results usually require hard endeavor. Finally, you may find that it will be advisable to plant your idea and let it grow, a matter that we deal with in the next chapter.

{17

How to Plant Your Idea and Make It Grow

Oɴᴇ ᴅᴀʏ I was talking with Max Levand, Wichita publisher, on what it takes to put a thing across. I commented that one of the most important is persistence. Scientist Galton, you may recall, included persistence as one of the elements making up genius.

Levand had been in the theater business and, with his movie programs, offered vaudeville acts. Along came Edgar Bergen in person. And what do you suppose happened? Levand recalled that when Edgar Bergen began his performances people would often get up and leave the theater. If Edgar Bergen had stopped right there, his story would have been a different one. The important point is that he didn't stop. His great build-up and big name were to come in later years.

The public mind gradually becomes accustomed to and even enthusiastic about certain things that it does not care for at first. The world is full of things that finally got there. Back in 1892, the J. I. Case Company built a gasoline tractor. But it was 20 years before such tractors received much recognition.

There was Doctor Long, down in Athens, Georgia, using ether for the first time as an anesthetic in 1842. But it was four long years before such a useful thing was elsewhere employed.

"Westinghouse perfected his airbrake before he was 30, but had to fight desperately, far into middle age, before he saw it recognized as one of the most important inventions of his time," Charles Kettering reminds us. "No one can say how many discoveries have been lost because the discoverers were not tough enough to stick to their guns and make the world believe. Young folks must realize that when a pioneer, through toil, thought and sweat, finds out how to make better airplanes or houses or surgical instruments his troubles really begin. They will then be stouter of heart and firmer of purpose, when they run into their own inevitable setbacks."

We have mentioned such difficulties before, but the question is: "What do you do in cases like this?"

One might, of course, keep batting away at a modest idea for a lifetime and then not see it a success. Sometimes, unfortunately, one does not know whether or not a project is worth while until the world accepts it.

Obviously, you would not want to waste a lifetime. Only superlative ideas deserve a lifetime. So may we make the suggestion that you plant your idea and let it grow for a while? But this does not mean that you are to bury the idea, unless you are ready to follow the example of the dog who digs the old bone up again to see if it is ready for eating.

This situation arises when your idea is too far ahead of the times or not in the immediate trend, or when your project is such a colossal one and so expensive that you cannot hope to "put it over" in just a few years.

Remember that the Christian religion was planted and has kept on growing for approximately 20 centuries. Shakespeare did not amount to more than an amusing scribbler in the judgment of his time. Jenner had a battle making people accept the thought of vaccination.

So, what you may do with many ideas is to carry them as far as you reasonably can at the moment. Then, every once in a while, you give them an extra push, as times become more propitious and as additional ideas for development and promotion are discovered.

If your project pays carrying charges and a modest income, well and good; if it doesn't, you may not desire to starve in the garret all the time. You can be working with other things while your pet idea matures.

Indeed our own work in creative thinking has been something of an experiment in planting and developing an idea in civilization. An aura of mystery had always been spread about the subject. People did not know how to do it or, more often, did not believe that it could be done.

It took a number of years to plant our idea and make it grow. But now that we have wrapped the package and delivered it to civilization, we have been amazed at the favorable reception. Where we used to receive one letter asking about it, today we receive a score. We seem to have won our little battle.

I have had a number of my ideas exceed anticipations. True, some failed, but parts of even many ideas that seemed unsuccessful came to life again and became valuable adjuncts of other ideas. Never throw away an idea completely. It may need only a different twist or another idea to help it out. And I only wish that I had stayed longer with some of my ideas. Later developments proved them to have been sound indeed.

Of all the men I have known, one of the most successful in taking what seemed like impossible ideas and giving them a build-up over the years was A. L. Gump of San Francisco. After the San Francisco earthquake had laid things flat, Mr. Gump was undecided. He had just about concluded that an art store was not for him, and he conceived the idea of the present supergrocery. Then he decided to stay with his original idea a while longer.

Just looking the whole matter over, who would have thought that rare things, particularly unknown and rare Oriental things, could have been generally popularized, even with prices in the ultrahigh brackets? "Some men in my line would like 30 top customers," Mr. Gump said to me one day. "I prefer 30,000."

He deliberately educated his customers. Mr. Gump would start with things that were unfamiliar to most—unfamiliar even to Mr. Gump—and before long he would be doing some financier a favor by letting him purchase them. Mr. Gump started with jade when it was hardly known in America and became one of the greatest jade merchants in the world. He liked some Imperial Chinese rugs, and soon he had the bright idea of having Chinese rugs made to order for his customers. One day a woman in Siam consigned to him a collection of stone figures. He had not any idea what they really were, and he and his assistants spent night after night puzzling over them. But finally he thought he knew enough to glamorize them, and they began to sell at stupendous prices. The lady who had originally shipped them had never thought much about them.

In talking with Mr. Gump, I tried to discover those factors that made him almost as much of an attraction in San Francisco as San Francisco itself. First, of course, he created the element of wonder—museum pieces right out in his shop for people to buy. And he had made an interesting adaptation, quite in accord with the principles laid down in this book, to do for Asiatic art what had already been done for European art. But the interesting point was that he kept adding new treasures to his stock. Once he had made a success in one field he could add another, and so make his original idea grow.

Mr. Gump gave everything a personalized build-up. He made his idea grow by talking about his treasures. It was the same principle as the lecturer's, but, instead of large audiences, he depended on individual lectures. Instead of hiding away in his office all day, he would be out walking about the store and promoting the idea of unusual things to possible customers one by one. "Take a look at these vases," he would say. "Feel them. Mr. So-and-so paid $100,000 for a pair of them, and I don't think his were really as good as these." In their minds he kindled the possibility of ownership. One day he found one of the richest women in America just leaning against a stairway in the store. In the course of

[235]

a few years, he educated her to the point of buying hundreds of thousands of dollars worth of goods.

What looks like an unusual use for a product is often highly successful later on when there are special circumstances that make its promotion easier. Who would ever have believed, for instance, that denim, the fabric favored by manual laborers, would advance into the high society of sports centers? It climbed in by the back window. Visitors at expensive dude ranches saw the cowhands attired in the coarsest of clothes. But the cowboy was a glamorous figure and thousands of young people wanting to imitate him cast aside their expensive riding habits and went in for blue pants and rough shirts. What can be said when the million-dollar heiress is wearing blue denim? It becomes a fashion.

But, likewise, what was once expensive and exclusive may degenerate. Corduroy, as its name implies, was once intended for kings but slid so far down the scale that it became a long-wearing cloth for manual labor. Then, later, it was rescued and moved up to bath robes and blouses.

George C. Quick of Phoenix used to be in the crop dusting business. He asked himself: "Why are there so many injurious plant insects today?" He had the answer, and also the remedy, in what became a profitable business in ladybugs. Wholesale land clearing, getting rid of wooded areas, and use of insecticides that destroy both good and bad bugs is the answer, he says. The balance is in favor of bad bugs today. Mr. Quick had played with ladybugs as a hobby. Then he saw that it could be made an interesting and profitable business because ladybugs are insects that eat other bugs but never touch a plant. That's the secret of selling ladybugs by the gallon to farmers and plant lovers who find that each ladybug can devour about 50 other bugs in a day.

Sometimes a man or business may want to stop the growing process in one direction and build in another. Often a man is confronted by the fact that he is recognized in only one field when, in reality, he wants to promote his other field of activity just as much, or maybe more. A man who was both a successful vocalist and a professor of education remarked to me one day: "I'm afraid I'm going to become recognized as a singer rather than as an authority on education. I want to be the authority on education." The trouble was that, when he went out to teachers' institutes and educational gatherings, he was too often hired "as the man who can lead the music." He dropped music.

The J. I. Case Company found itself confronted with much the same problem. Because it had so long been recognized as a leader in the steam engine and threshing field, there was implanted in the public mind the thought that it did not concern itself with other implements. But, in the twenties, it began to make many other implements, and it was a major task to sell the public on the fact that it made them. It accomplished the task by the repeated emphasis in its advertising of the phrase "77 Modern Farm Machines." In later years, of course, it increased that number, but the ice had been broken in turning from a tractor and threshing company to an implement company.

Bigger and Better Than You Dreamed

After you have got things going in one direction, it is time to try that practice of the research departments of the great corporations: deciding how *you* may grow in another direction. The map of industrial success points in all directions. All ideas have to grow, yours as well as those of the great corporation. Maybe the side possibilities will turn sure financial defeat into sure financial success.

Perhaps you thought you failed but really succeeded. Perkin discovered coal-tar dyes. But it was a side issue; he was searching for artificial quinine. Then there was the discoverer of carborundum. In the midst of another experiment, he found a tiny bit of material of unusual hardness. It cut anything, it seemed. I have missed things, even after they were going fairly well, because I did not discern that there were greater possibilities than I had sensed or planned for at the beginning.

Look and look some more! Does your invention or idea have greater possibilities than you thought? Are there other hidden uses? Is there an entirely different market? Could you change the thing and triple its sales possibilities? In corporations, many groups of people get together on ideas. Sometimes a weak idea, through someone's suggestion, is given just the touch that makes it succeed.

Universal principles always have different applications. You find that the principle works in one place, so why not in another? John Tigrett of "drinking duck" fame invented the Zoomerang, a toy in another field which shoots a projectile on a plastic paper strip from a miniature gun. Tigrett wondered why the same idea could not be used to shoot arrows and invented another toy. He thinks so highly of his duck that continually bobs its head for a drink of water that he seeks to control it by 20 patents because of the extra possibilities that he senses.

[238]

Years ago, when I began working with the principles laid down in this book, I felt that possibly the greatest application would be in the field of writing. The reason was that I had seen the need for ideas in journalism students. I gave some attention to invention. But interestingly enough, a tremendous demand developed among men in business, who saw that we had universal and not isolated principles. Here were the presidents and vice presidents of great corporations telephoning, telegraphing, and writing for what we had to offer. They had seen more quickly than any other single group the monetary rewards that come to people with ideas.

Anyone who has traveled in California or Florida knows the drug stores that display their "orange juice, toast, and coffee" signs promptly at 8 o'clock in the morning. But what I saw in Texas was more impressive, for, in a Dallas drugstore, I found a veritable smallpox outbreak of signs extolling the merits of orange drinks. Such concoctions as peach sundaes and strawberry sodas rated only one banner, but here were oranges with eight or nine streamers.

There were just plain old-fashioned orangeades and orange sherbets for the cautious stomach. For the most experienced orange drinker, an orange cooler with a bit of sherbet was suggested. But most exciting of all was an orange melody, described on a yellow banner as the coolest drink in town, made of orange juice, syrup, milk, and ice, beaten up and delivered to you in a cocktail shaker.

There was at hand a pretty Texas waitress all ready to do the right thing in case anyone should have the termerity to order a chocolate sundae. She looked me over very doubtfully, much as a bartender would upon giving a boy a bottle of pop. Of course, I didn't have the earmarks of a seasoned

[239]

orange toper. She finally said: "You know, we've got just plain orange juice, too."

I got myself in hand and ordered the melody. The waitress was impressed: "You're not in the orange business, are you?" And, my dear Californians, those were Texas oranges.

What many businesses are trying to do is to get out of the seasonal slump. Schick razors were originally sold largely as a gift item at Christmas. But then Schick began advertising razors not merely as a gift but as something to be purchased by a man himself any time of the year. Sometimes one may actually turn the tide by suggesting why the commodity should be purchased in what would otherwise be a dull season.

The most important examples of turning liabilities into assets are evident in the fashionable winter resorts that are now exerting themselves to secure summer tourists and among the summer places seeking winter visitors. Money obtained in that way is just so much velvet. An example of this sort is Santa Barbara, California. I can remember the time when that city conceived of itself solely as a place for the rich winter visitor. When summer came around, hotels were all but closed, shopkeepers took siestas for a month or so, and everyone waited for the "season." Now, thanks to the development of the beach and bathing facilities along the shore, more people think of Santa Barbara as a summer resort than as a winter one. You may actually stay at some fashionable hotels there at a lower rate in the winter than in the summer. California now emphasizes that it is an all-year tourist resort.

Florida and the West Indies are selling the summer advantages of their seasides. Miami Beach has a real summer season, growing year by year, and most of the beach hotels are crowded.

Thousands of small businesses have a capacity for great growth. Sam Gorelnick sensed the possibilities of a shoe repair and shine shop in San Antonio. Then he decided that there must be many people outside of San Antonio who wanted something done for their shoes. So out went men into the surrounding country inquiring why Sam Gorelnick could not do business by mail, how many had heard of him, and, if not, why not? Soon as much business was coming from outside as from the town itself.

Then he wondered if there were not other things that people wanted done besides shining and soling. He established a unique "breaking in" department for new shoes. "You know, the big thing about the whole shoe repair business is that people want the comfort of the old shoe with the neatness of the new," he told me. "They have their old shoes fixed because they are so comfortable. We renew everything but the pinch. People do not like new shoes because they generally don't fit. So they bring them here to be fitted." Then he discovered a new formula for dyeing shoes. And soon people were asking him to make shoes by hand.

Joseph Kolodny envisions and promotes a new type of general store, not the old store, the crossroads store, or the old-time corner tobacco store but one where the merchandise is as varied as the ideas of the proprietor. Everything from tobacco to men's shirts now finds a place in his type of store.

The extra bright idea is the one that pays off. Ralph Snider of Hamilton, Ohio, developed a sideline by using the telephone to sell Christmas fruit cakes in large lots to business executives for Christmas presents. Jack Conrad started a cigaret lighter hospital in his store.

Ideas have to keep growing while they are in their early stages. You never know how big they'll grow later. There was *Rudolph the Red-Nosed Reindeer,* the underdog deer who got his nose into all sorts of money-making endeavors. He was created by Robert L. May, an advertising writer for Montgomery Ward. Once upon a time, May's boss told him to get up an animal story. For his Cinderella, May decided on a poor little Rudolph, a reindeer with a big red nose who was always being laughed at by the other reindeer because he did not have a nose like theirs. But Rudolph was finally rescued—and by whom, do you suppose? Old Santa Claus put him right at the head of all the reindeer pulling the sleigh. You see his nose was so bright and shiny that it cut through the gloom all over the world and Santa Claus then could find everyone who deserved a present.

May tested the story on his little daughter, Barbara, who liked it. Montgomery Ward presented 2,500,000 copies to its customers back in 1939. Then Rudolph had to sleep during the war when Santa couldn't make presents so well, but, in 1946, 3,500,000 copies were again handed out.

The next year Sewell Avery, the head of Montgomery Ward, decided that May should have copyright and royalties on Rudolph. A publisher sold 100,000 copies of the story, and Rudolph began to have his likeness on slippers, picture puzzles, sweat shirts, and stuffed toys. Then the number of books swept on upward, and Rudolph got his nose into everything from music to watches to toy banks.

You, too, may plant your idea and see it grow. You may,

of course, plant a great number of ideas and have a veritable orchard of bright projects that keep maturing over the years. You will water them, prune them, and graft them. Some will die, but others, let us hope, will mature successfully.

18

How Versatile Dare You Be?

CHAUCER was a collector of customs. Benjamin Franklin was a printer. Mendel, geneticist, was abbot of a monastery. Priestley, the discoverer of oxygen, was a preacher.

Alexander Borodin of Russia was a chemist, physician, and composer. Bernard Palissy was a glass painter, portrait painter, and surveyor who became a famous potter. On the other hand, William De Morgan was a famous potter and at the mature age of 65 changed over and became a highly successful novelist.

Sir Arthur Conan Doyle was a student, whaler, country physician, author, war correspondent. Sir Arthur was not just the creator of Sherlock Holmes; he won his knighthood for *The Great Boer War*.

A. P. Giannini, California banker, was a commission merchant. He had made enough money at 31 years of age to retire on a modest income. But he didn't like the way banking was being conducted; so he stepped over into the banking business and became one of the famous bankers of the world.

Sir Winston Churchill won the Nobel prize in literature. But, just looking at his record, one would have placed the emphasis in his career not on literature but on government.

My old teacher, Walter B. Pitkin, was a famous Columbia professor who did many interesting things. He loved change and, once one field was conquered, he started for another. At one time, he was considered an authority on short stories. But not long before his death, he remarked to me, "I don't believe I've read a story through for five years." He had been a farmer, one of the principal editors of the *Encyclopedia Britannica,* and a consultant for moving picture companies. He built a new type of boat and nearly lost his life trying it. He pioneered in a half dozen new fields in education. In him was always the spirit of mental adventure.

Cyrus W. Field was ready to retire from a paper business with a comfortable fortune at 34 years of age. But he had the idea of a trans-Atlantic telegraph. A bold, daring idea it was. To us, looking backwards, it seems commonplace, but then it was strange to think of laying a cable along the ocean floor.

Harrington Emerson, the great leader of the efficiency movement in American business, taught modern languages at a midwestern college.

Leonardo da Vinci is perhaps the classic example in history of a man who changed repeatedly the direction of his life. He was a supreme artist, an engineer, a pioneer in sci-

[245]

ence, and a city planner. He seemed to be a success in everything.

How topsy-turvy can we get? Lest this seem like quite a mix-up, let us recall that modern corporations are becoming quite as versatile as these gifted individuals. International Telephone and Telegraph sells refrigerators; General Mills turns out flat irons; Parker Pen sells cigaret lighters; Holly Sugar has oil wells; General Motors turns out locomotives; United States Steel builds houses; United States Leather, for some years until its dissolution, was not in leather but in natural gas. Drug stores sell groceries, and now, to turn the tables, the chain groceries sell drugs.

Can anybody do everything?

How versatile can *you* be? Or rather, how versatile dare *you* be? Are you to be like John Tigrett, successful toy manufacturer, who has been a book salesman, hotel operator, real estate operator, oil well driller, bus company officer, navy lieutenant, and investment counsellor?

One side of the mind seems to say: "I'm not happy. I want a change. That new line of work looks good. Think I'll go ahead."

But the other side of the mind seems to say: "Whoa! Better stay back where you are and let well enough alone. This changing about isn't for you. Don't be a jack-of-all-trades."

And both sides of your mind ask me: "What about it?"

Versatility consists in doing a great number of things, often unrelated, and doing them well. I should like to add that versatile men and women have a great number of good ideas as well as the gumption to see those ideas through to success.

Now one of the significant points in connection with this

[246]

matter of creativity is that creation in everything seems to be fundamentally the same. Professor L. L. Thurstone would say: "Let us begin with the working hypothesis that creative talent is qualitatively the same at all levels: in the trades and in the professions, as well as in the rare and extreme forms that we call genius."

A well-known company engaged in engineering one day called me long distance to ask if I would attend a conference dealing with creative thought in that corporation. "But I'm not an engineer," I answered.

"We know that," was the reply, "but you have the overall picture of things."

To one who has been reading this book it will be evident that creation consists in shifting an infinite number of attributes from one thing to another, whether it be in creating a doodad for the dime store or a painting for the art gallery. It is all the same process. Consequently a man able to create rapidly in one field ought to be able to create rapidly in another.

But it is not as simple as that. There is complexity of background and technical accomplishment in many fields of activity. One has to have knowledge of what he may profitably adapt. Of course, occasionally a man comes along without prior experience, as Howe did with the sewing machine. He threw the accepted manner of sewing out the window and started a new stitch. And it is likewise possible, as was the case with Bell, for one to start right out and acquire the technical knowledge, even though today that becomes a Herculean undertaking in many fields.

So we may add something to our position here. A man may be as versatile as he desires, providing that he is willing to acquire the background of the field in which he intends to operate. Or his ideas may be so revolutionary that he upsets that entire background. Many modern artists have done the latter.

One of the very great automobile designers does not draw. He never learned how. He has a great staff of artists working under him, and he simply explains what he wants. He is primarily an idea man and secured his position because the head of an automobile company happened to see a stunning car the man had put together by himself.

When depression days struck America, Ernest Henderson and Robert L. Moore salvaged $25,000 from their radio business and, starting with one bright idea, became among the largest hotel proprietors in the world. Henderson and Moore saw that hotels needed ideas. Many of them had fallen into the hands of insurance companies and mortgage interests that had not had much experience in the hotel business. Neither had Henderson and Moore. But they gathered up enough ideas to carry them through.

The one big bright idea was to buy up hotels that had so many mortgages and other obligations that the common stock or control could be had for next to nothing. Then they began to put in ideas to build up the hotels into profitable institutions. They began to decorate, air condition, utilize all waste space, operate their own concessions in the hotels, cut costs by new methods, make it simple to secure a hotel reservation, and advertise. They even maintained an experimental kitchen for the creation of new things to eat. Their group of hotels is now the Sheraton chain.

One of the most interesting men ever to walk up and down the halls of the old library building at the University of Nebraska was a professor of literature, C. W. Wallace. He was interested in Shakespeare. He liked to go to London and browse around. The only thing that seemed to prevent his doing it all the time—as a sort of permanent occupation—was lack of money.

He got to thinking it over. A conscientious gentleman, one day he calmly announced to his associates: "I've thought it all over, and I feel that I would do the world the least harm by going down to Texas and making money in oil." And off he went.

We used to hear varied stories. Some said he had made it. Others said he hadn't. But one day I happened to be in Fort Worth talking with an officer of a great oil company. "Oh, yes, he made it," the oil man remarked. "We offered him a million dollars twelve years after he came down here, and he turned us down."

Wallace demonstrated that not only could he assemble the knowledge and background of the oil business but that he could keep a few jumps ahead of the other men. He got his start by an interesting piece of observation. He found a piece of land between the holdings of two major oil companies. Each company thought the other oil company controlled it. But when the professor's eagle eye saw that neither had it, he acquired the rights.

He also learned to be a contrary thinker, which is usually creative problem solving to a high degree. "I recall," said the oil executive, "how many times he did what he was told not to do and then came out on top."

There is a very important and profitable point that most people fail to see in connection with versatility. That is the fact that versatility exists to a very great degree in connec-

[249]

tion with almost any field of work. The fundamental background may be much the same.

Some years ago George Sokolsky, the columnist, and I were out driving. The times were still not altogether happy ones—we were in the depression—yet Mr. Sokolsky told me that he could not think of a single journalism graduate in his class at Columbia University who was then making less than $10,000 a year. The interesting fact I learned was that they had not all remained in newspaper work, but they were off in the related fields. Men and women can make wonderful progress by developing ideas that take them over into related fields. Several journalists became bankers via the route of public relations. One built a great publishing house because he saw the opportunity of adapting crossword puzzles from newspapers to books. The most successful journalists have often been men who did not remain routine journalists; they moved over into politics. The journalist possesses the background for many fields.

If you will recall some of the figures whose names appeared at the beginning of this chapter, you will note that much of their diversity was in related fields. Take the case of John Buchan, who, before he became Baron Tweedsmuir and Governor General of Canada, was a novelist, essayist, poet, lawyer, soldier, businessman, and member of parliament. It is readily apparent that novelist, historian, essayist, and poet are related fields. Being a lawyer and a member of parliament are related. Most men have been a soldier at some time, and we all have to be businessmen to some degree.

Christian Dior, the famous *couturier* of Paris, wanted to be a composer or an architect. He ran an art gallery, but he ended up as a designer of women's clothes. His employees will tell you, "We don't sell clothes, we sell ideas." So if you are thinking in terms of successful versatility, explore the versatility that exists in your own basic line of work.

Shall We Take a Chance?

How big a chance shall we take? A natural question.

Most people do take chances and have always taken them, as witness the gambling craze today and through the ages. It is not entirely a matter of the possibility of getting something for nothing. There is the feeling of being proved right in judgment, or of winning out against odds. We all seem to have this adventurous instinct.

Most of us feel that we have little chance to adventure. So we take a chance at the lottery. Out-and-out gambling has its bad feature in wasting a tremendous amount of time in dreaming of a future of seldom realized profits. I am not worried particularly over the matter of someone's now and then winning a little money. But gambling takes away the zest for other things in life. My main criticism is that it makes no contribution to the progress or well-being of the average individual or the country.

But this "take a chance" idea suggests that people (all of us, in fact) are interested in such things. What we can do is to take some chances on ourselves. There are plenty of adventures in real life and real business that are more exciting than any gambling one ever enjoyed. But, quite rightly, what we seek to do is to avoid getting in too deep.

You may have noticed that many individuals taking chances have been men amply able to take risks. They had money back of them. But, looking at it in another way, the man most able to take a risk may be one who can lose little if things go against him.

A young man may well adventure before he marries and settles down. If you are off to a bad start, there is nothing like a change, nothing like creating new events to make you happy again. College and university students should break with their environment when things are not going well. I have thanked my lucky stars many times that I got out of certain environments. Maybe you have done the same.

The president of a great university once told me that the best thing that can happen to a young man or woman is to have to change around from one thing to another several times during his twenties. When you look over those who have "stuck," you will find that many of them have stayed ten, fifteen, or twenty years in almost the same positions with no increases in opportunity. Those changing around have finally turned up with the good jobs.

One of my most interesting students was a young woman who specialized in journalism at the University of Nebraska, Kate Goldstein, later Mrs. Kay Kamen. No sooner did she get out of school than she was off to New York to open her own publicity organization. But it was not so long before we began to hear interesting rumors that Kate the journalist was becoming a well-known leather designer. One day I asked a designer who knows all about such things. "Oh, yes, indeed," he replied, "she is one of the three great leather designers." An airplane crash in the Azores, when she was returning from Paris, cut short a brilliant career.

Among my students during the past 15 years who afterwards made names for themselves have been many we might term adventurers. They are the individuals with their own books in the store windows; they are the ones with the two-hundred-a-week jobs; they are the boys and girls at the mahogany desks. They stirred around, turned up in unusual parts of the world, and, all in all, had a whale of a time. Generally the records have been made by the adventurers.

The other day I picked up a paper with a half-page story about a woman whose bid to fame was that she had taught over 50 years in one locality. But, just being fair about the matter, wouldn't it have been better for her to have had some fun? Thousands of people at home are vagrants quite as much as the man on the road. Instead of lacking the courage to settle down, they lack the courage to stir around.

But—

How are you going to know if you are the sort of individual who dares take a chance with his versatility? Well, I think one of the tests is right before you. If you are one overflowing with bright and useful ideas, then the versatile road may well be the one for you. But if you find idea production difficult, it would be best not to consider it.

That is the message of versatility. Ideas, you have learned, let you travel in any direction. There is nothing to prevent anyone from doing anything providing he can make it work successfully and make other people like it. But in order to know *what* to adapt, you may have to explore many fields. The more things you know about, the greater the possibilities of creation—for you can acquire more ideas with which to build. That is the value of being an explorer. But if you cannot go far afield, remember that the possibilities of exploring within your own line are tremendous.

19

Ideas Can Keep You and Your Business Young

I wish i were ten years younger."

"If I only had my life to live over again."

"The past five years have gone faster than any other five years in my life. They have flitted by almost without my knowing it. *I'm getting older.*"

How often we hear those words! They are about as significant as any within our hearing. Time is steadily pursuing itself around the clock. This day will never come again! It shocks us and quite rightly.

Time is a mystery. To you, sitting there reading this, it may not appear to be so at first thought. Your watch ticks off the seconds and the hours, the sun rises and sets, and that seems to be all there is to it.

Let us say that, Sunday, you returned from a trip down

south. You spent only a week away from home, but it seems that you went everywhere. You got that big order at Hot Springs, Arkansas, and then, as a reward for yourself, you tried the famous baths. Down to New Orleans, where that store gave you a wonderful idea for a new product. Over to Houston, where you found your apartment house doing better than you thought it would. Coming home, you suddenly decided to travel around by way of Natchez, Mississippi, and seek an adventure into the historic past. Finally, home again. You look back, and it seems ages since you left home, but in reality it was only a week.

Again, you are reading history. Here you are in the Civil War. And it has taken well on to a hundred pages. What a long drawn-out affair! But you keep reading along, and the first thing you know you are at the panic of the nineties. Twenty-five years of relative peace in America have taken up less space than five years of war. Again you have been deceived on this matter of time, or, rather, the history book seems to have been deceived.

Time—what is it? We sit in our chair and count the hours. It may be four hours by the clock, but we may think it only two hours or as much as six hours. The bear, hibernating in his cave, feels its passage not at all.

Just a while ago, this matter of time was, oh, so simple. It was a quarter past three; you were 30 years old; the day was 24 hours long; the world had moved 25 years in the past quarter of a century; all was definite and precise. Now you are not so sure.

The average individual has probably accepted time much as he accepted the earth and the sun—as something to be taken for granted. We have been acquiring our conceptions of time much as we would the letters of the alphabet. It is said that the idea of morning and night does not come to three-fourths of all children until four years of age; the conception of today, yesterday, and tomorrow at six years; and of clock time, not until eight years.

Time, as we have generally understood it, is opposed to each one of us, and we are opposed to it. We fight time. Time fights us. We fight time because we think that this solar system of ours has something to do with our growing old. Time fights us because the laws of the sun and stars are not our laws.

But, when you look at time in another way, you find that this is not entirely necessary. Why should we be in such anxiety to make our time that of the heavens, which, after all, is not our time at all?

Clock time is simply a meeting place. We say that we are going to meet at Dupont Circle, and we fix the place. We say at three o'clock, and that's the hour; otherwise we should wander around and maybe not meet the other person at all. When the sun and stars are in a certain position, we shall do thus and so. But, when we make solar time more than simply a bookkeeping transaction, we fail. Our future is not that of the heavens. The sun and the stars go on their way quite unconcerned about us.

Empty time is inconceivable. *Events happening within it give us the sense of the passage of time.* Without these things happening, life would seem to remain stationary. It would be much like space without any objects in it. Time is an empty shell into which you put things, just as space is an empty shell into which you put people and buildings and houses and pieces of the world itself.

[256]

We speak of time flitting by, but is it *time* that moves? What keeps turning the past and the present into the future? It is *change* in us and in our surroundings. Time becomes a moving picture of many things in the process of change.

Events tell time much more accurately than the clock and calendar.

The greatest event is that of being born. The next greatest is that of death. In between are all sorts of events. Taken together they make up time and life.

And what is the nature of these events? Some of them occur within our own bodies; others are brought to pass by natural law. Some are imposed upon us by forces within the world, by aggregations of men. But many of them we bring to pass ourselves.

The Expanding Circle of Events

One of the remarkable things about these important events is that the "newness" of them to us often determines their significance.

To most of us, a visit to Paris *is* an event. It will be indelibly registered in our memory, and two or three days looking around will seem like as many weeks. But suppose that we have been spending all the summer or winter in Paris. After the first two or three weeks, the days will gather speed, and if we sit down and actually live in Paris, the days may finally shorten their length in our recollection as they shorten themselves anywhere else; that is, unless we continually pour *new* things into them.

It is rather apparent that if we had Christmas every week like Sunday, it would fail to have the same significance that it possesses coming only once a year. If we were guides instead of tourists in the Canadian Rockies, mountain climbs would not seem the big things that they do.

This search after newness is one of the most valuable characteristics of the human spirit. It accounts for the expansion of man and his world. It helps us to grow from youngsters to adult men and women. It makes and keeps us young.

Take a pencil and draw a circle. In the very center of this circle put a dot. That is you, just born. It's a wonderful world, full of new things. The very simplest of them are marvellous. Everything is unique. You're interested in many things to which adults never give so much as a thought. You lie and coo at that bit of red glass as if it were the biggest ruby ever discovered. Your circle of things is a small but entrancing one.

But, finally, you get a little older. You are more sophisticated at one year of age. You do not look at that ruby glass with the same enthusiasm. You are out exploring new things: the greens, blues, and yellows in the carpet; that new mug out of which you sip your milk; what happens when you upset the milk; those clothes you wear; and many, many other things. Your circle is expanding.

By five, you are looking around the world in a big way. Not content with exploring at home, you may even venture on occasion to run away from home. Kindergarten introduces the school days, and then come reading and writing, all sorts of schoolmates, moving pictures, ice cream sodas and sundaes, and glimpses now and then of the great world beyond your town.

So much to see, and do, and think. High school and

maybe college, and these new things always keep coming with a rush. Life—bright, new, cheerful, and delightful.

Your early years, then, are long, very long. There are so many new things that you keep discovering, there are many changes within yourself. Every day you are a Christopher Columbus. Every month you take possession of vast empires.

But just when did you stop being a Christopher Columbus? What a funny question that is! The chances are you *did* stop, and that is one thing the matter with you, the matter with all of us. The matter with our businesses, too.

Take a look at your circle again. It's more than just a circle; there are many circles within the big circle. It didn't take a big circle in those early years to give the feeling of breadth and length of life. But the farther along we got, the wider and broader our experiences had to be.

But, finally, what happened? *We settled down.* And when that happened, time began increasingly to run away with us. Life was no longer new; it became colorless and drab; there was no longer an expanding circle. From about the age of 30 on, there was a great void of empty space, space into which events no longer were placed, in which nothing happened.

In reality, our circle might go on expanding. There is no fundamental cause why it should not. There is a very good reason why it should.

"Those who have learned the secret of perpetual youth have learned to remain children at heart," asserts Dr. Frank S. Caprio.

Events Are Made by Ideas

And what is an event but an idea that someone has translated into action? Usually the more important the idea, the more important the event. *Events are the realization of ideas.* Some are but tiny ideas, ideas that have their sparkle and then wink out with the coming of more important things. Some are great revolutionary ideas. The world is being constantly made and remade by ideas and the events that they engender.

Of course, events and ideas measure the lives of corporations just as they do the lives of individuals. You know many a company of which it can be said, "They haven't had a bright idea in 25 years." Then along comes a new competitor with just a few bright ideas, and soon the older company is in the background.

I recall one such astonishing case when a small shopping newspaper became such a success that it actually made the old-time paper sell out to it. "It isn't the years that make us old but the old ideas we persist in carrying around with us," says Carl Holmes.

Business is becoming so competitive today that its executives have to keep both themselves and their companies youthful by the idea route. Developments are coming so rapidly that any concern without ideas would become old in almost no time. Take radio and television, for example. Motorola was founded as the Galvin Manufacturing Company with $565 in capital. In a quarter of a century, it had reached yearly sales of more than $200,000,000. "But," says President Paul Galvin, "we have scarcely scratched our pos-

[260]

sibilities." The company is not only receptive to ideas, it puts its foremen and superintendents in the way of picking them up. It is constantly sending them on tours to see what ideas other companies are using in their lines.

We have to give ourselves a going over—repackage ourselves, as it were—just as Rexall did with its drugs. Once the Rexall Company carried out a program of redesigning packages on 5,000 different items in 20 lines. The sales appeal of the different products had to be made outstanding, just as an individual may have to improve his personal appeal.

"It's true that an insurance company must have the policies, the people and the facilities for providing insurance protection," remarked President Frazar B. Wilde of the Connecticut General Life Insurance Company. "But it cannot live on these alone. It needs something more for healthy growth. It needs ideas and it needs a pioneering spirit to carry out these ideas. Yes, ideas have been our tradition. It was on ideas that Connecticut General was founded. It was on ideas that we have steadily grown. It will be on ideas that our future rests."

Ideas and events rejuvenate both individuals and corporations. Alexis Carrel called this, rejuvenation *by a happy event*. Two men were staying in an old people's home in Illinois. But suddenly oil was discovered on their farms. "You should have seen them get up and get out of that home," their niece remarked to me.

Every once in a while you see this type of rejuvenation. It may have been a long time since you have seen a certain man. But here he is now, alert, vigorous, and up-and-coming. "Things have happened to him," you say, quite rightly. He's done something big. His event has been important enough to change everything.

"Young men nowadays seem to want their careers made to order," remarked the great publisher, Cyrus H. K. Curtis, "when we can see from the lives of all successful men that the only careers worth having are those we carve for ourselves."

Vernon Pick was a modern-day prospector, not for gold but for uranium. To start with, he didn't know much about uranium. His electrical supply store in Minneapolis had burned down, and he did not have enough money to go back into business. Adventuring in his pick-up truck, he heard about uranium strikes in the Rockies. He asked the Atomic Energy Commission, "How and where do you prospect?" He learned about a remote section of Utah. After months of traveling by truck and foot, he found a great outcropping right in the open. In a few months he had taken out hundreds of thousands of dollars worth of ore. Now all of us can't go and look for uranium, but this experience illustrates the battle and the reward.

To promote youthfulness in his company, President Austin S. Igleheart of Generals Foods prunes the company as he would a fruit tree. The basic idea is to build up a profitable corporation by adding lines that will make substantial profits and eliminating those that do not do too well. General Foods has gone into research and development in a big way. In seven years, sales of new products have represented seven times the money spent on research. Sometimes interesting things just happen. One day a cousin of the King of Afghanistan walked in carrying a stove. He put it on the desk of R. M. Schmitz, vice president in charge of new products, and prepared a bowl of rice in just half the time the housewife usually spends on such a task. General Foods did not let him get away until it had the rights to a thing like that.

The Rockefeller brothers are trying the bold plan of rejuvenating parts of the world by ideas and events. It is an experiment in using money to achieve social and economic progress as well as a fair return on their investment. They are venturing everywhere. They are manufacturing cotton textiles in the Belgian Congo; they are developing inexpensive housing through new building ideas in America; they are seeking to produce cheaper food in Venezuela. When an enterprise is on its feet, they take out their original investment; when it fails, they write off their loss.

Youth Can Come Later

There is additional encouragement for those who are growing older in clock years. Youth today comes later. To take a great creative step in civilization often requires more preparation than it once did. Not all the simple things have been invented and not all the simple discoveries have been made, but most discoveries and creative works do require some background on which to build. You may be a champion runner when young and a great philosopher when old.

While psychologists used to say that chemists did their best work between 28 and 32, inventors between 31 and 35 and "men of letters" between 38 and 42, I doubt very much that such will be the case in the future. Many men are just ready to start at those ages. It is probably only surplus energy that enables the youngster to appear more creative.

[263]

The older individuals have far more on which to build, once they learn the process. Milton wrote *Paradise Lost* at 50 years of age. Luigi Cornaro at 95 showed Venice how to reclaim waste land. Commodore Vanderbilt did most of his railroad building after 70 and is said to have added a hundred millions to his fortune.

A woman famous for her ideas, Dorothy Canfield Fisher, came to visit our university. It was over 40 years from the day she had left our college town as a high school graduate until the day she returned to lecture. Imagine our astonishment when she notified us that she would arrive on the express at 2:15 A.M.; give her lecture in the morning at 10 o'clock; attend a noon luncheon; look around the city and university in the afternoon; and make a speech at a banquet that evening. Then she would take the train again, at 11:30 that night. Why, it made young fellows sleepy just to look at a schedule like that.

But the stranger thing was this: It was a very young woman who hopped off the train that night at 2:15!

One day a man asked a Japanese how old his father was. Told that that gentleman, a painter, was in the eighties, the questioner commented, "He doesn't look that old."

"Of course not," the Japanese answered. "An artist lives a long time. He has something to think about besides himself."

What have some long-lived men to say about this?

Edwin Markham, at 83: "Even at 100 one is old only if he thinks he is old. Man's useless period is reached when he begins to live in the past. . . ."

George Bernard Shaw: "I am not distinguished by having

[264]

birthdays. Man is a complex of parts, no two of which reach their prime on the same date."

William Lyon Phelps: "A person is not old until his thoughts turn more to the past than to the present or future."

Frank H. Vizetelly: "Advancing years can have no terrors for those whose minds are occupied."

Samuel Untermeyer: "It is a grand thing for a man to keep fully occupied and so forget all about his diminishing span."

Holding back the years is more than simply living to be men and women old in years. There have been many books aiming at longer life, more actual years, through conservation of one's health. But unfortunately, many of these conserving oldsters are really going to die young, young in the sense that their event years have been far too short—much shorter than they ever needed to be.

Lengthening Each Day

But here comes a natural question. You say to me, "I don't care about big, world-smashing ideas and events. What about these smaller things? Aren't little ideas to be counted just as much as very striking money-making ones?"

And I answer, "Yes." There are thousands of little ideas that come bubbling along through the course of life, and they serve an interesting purpose, that of lengthening one's existence. That is where they fit into our picture, in rejuvenating life.

What can you do for the smaller units of time, the days and hours, to make them sparkle? You can seek greater significance in each individual day. This is important even for the man or woman who seeks greater events in life. The result will be the same in degree, and small events may lead to great ones. Try a few of the following prescriptions:

1. A new schedule in anything tends to lengthen time. For instance, try the fun of getting up early some morning and of going somewhere. What a long day you will have. Readjust your living plan. Most evenings are spent in triviality. Try moving your dinner hour to seven or seven-thirty as on the Continent. Use that hour or hour and a half of daylight for outdoor recreation. You cannot then say that you have no time for it. Twilight is the most enjoyable hour. This is the same principle that the architect uses in design. By placing many things in a small space, he gives the impression that the space itself is really much larger than it is. You place things in time instead of space.

2. Get over into some new fields of thought. The shelves of your library or bookstore will suggest dozens of such fields. But remember that this thought should go somewhere. There should be an end, an aim to be accomplished. Better have some aim that must be changed occasionally than no aim at all. Think up some bright new thing to do every week: music, art, recreation, almost any *new* thing will have this time-lengthening effect.

3. The rapidity with which bright, new, profitable ideas sparkle into the mind will actually lengthen an afternoon or even a day. If you do not believe this, try the experiment of dilly-dallying away an afternoon on nothing. Then, on the next day, spend your afternoon on several things where there can be sparkling ideas and some evidence of accomplishment. You will find a great difference. The afternoon

on which I have been writing this immediate paragraph has proved a long successful one to me, because so many miscellaneous things have been done.

4. Turn some commonplace events into real ones. It is possible to magnify many small events. Many things deserve to be magnified through more careful preparation. Take a Maine Christmas, for example. Those New Englanders smelled the plum pudding and mince pies for weeks ahead. Contrast it with the hurried preparation most of us know. Instead of having Christmas descend upon you like a flashing meteor, try spreading it out. In parts of Europe, that is a common custom. Christmas lasts more than a month. It begins about December fifth, when Santa Claus arrives with small gifts. It takes time to work up to the real Christmas. And, finally, it is not over until well after New Year's. Start your Christmas shopping earlier. Distribute some of the events of holiday week into the earlier parts of December and January.

5. In your daily work, try varying ideas and changes in procedure instead of bogging down on the same plan all the time. You do not need to walk or drive to work the same way every morning; you may not need to do everything each day in the same order. It is difficult to produce new things when slaves to routine. Business houses often think they are on the alert when all they are doing is shuffling papers. Emmet J. Leahy asserts that, in banks and insurance companies, 52 per cent of employees handle papers rather than produce new business. In textiles, 26 per cent do the same. In the chemical industry, it is 16 per cent. Business may be burdened down by routine living quite as much as the individual.

Reporting a statement by a Tokyo professor that large numbers of people are mentally unbalanced, the *Nippon Times* seconds his suggestion of the need of frequent breaks in the monotony of an impoverished existence to give stimulus and enjoyment. Ideas and events furnish zest to life and business.

Life seems to need side issues. And there are many pathways to them. "Two keys to human happiness are the right of man to create his own ideas, or works of art, or materials of commerce, and the right of man to exchange all these things with his fellow men," declares Dr. R. G. Gustavson.

"It is said that everyone should have a hobby," remarks B. O. Austin, well-known Westinghouse electrical engineer with over 40 patents that have actually been put to use. "Many think that so long as it is a hobby of some sort the situation is satisfied. But there is a difference in hobbies. Most hobbies involve the act of acquiring. They have very little creative activity connected with them.

"One of the outstanding creative hobbies of today is the home workshop. It may range from research of the highest order to the making of the lowly wedge for holding a door open. I think this activity deserves a better name. It should be called the 'Home Creative Laboratory.' The laboratory does not have to follow any set pattern. It may be based on any creative activity. Today it is generally thought of as a place for the handicrafts. This need not be true. It may be devoted to advertising, writing, the arts, economics, plant life, animal life, chemistry, research, science, engineering, and other activities where creative effort can be exercised."

Many a man could tell you that it was his sideline that saved him from disaster. But more than that, these somewhat more modest adventures may often be pursued right in your own business. What interesting opportunities there are for new methods of selling things and new things to sell! There is no greater thrill sometimes than carrying out a simple matter such as a bit of direct mail promotion. Then, from morning to morning, watch the postman bring back the replies. Even if you lose some money here occasionally, you will be more than repaid in learning at first hand just what brings in the returns and what doesn't. If you are master of your own time in a business, try taking a few hours for developing new ideas. If you are an ordinary employee, use whatever spare time you have on the job for trying new ideas.

These things do not always require money, but they do require a certain degree of management. Best of all, small ideas and events may lead to big ones. If you are still in doubt about producing that important event, make up some questions for yourself. What used to be your ambition? What is it that you have always wanted to do and at which you've never taken a chance? Are you still a "wish I were" individual? Answering such questions, as we suggested earlier in this book, will bring to light plenty of things. Few, so very few, people have ever achieved their early ambitions. And there are few people who have not some things in mind at which they would like to try their hands. Try one of them for a sideline.

And don't forget to refer to that little notebook of ideas that you have been keeping all the while you have been reading this book. You may find there just the idea you need for brightening your life by the idea route.

"Personal satisfaction and happiness come from the inside

by your own efforts," says B. O. Austin. "This being true, then our greatest satisfaction and happiness come directly from what we do with our imagination. The greatest tonic on earth for the 'blues' or being 'fed up' is to accomplish something of which you are proud and which is warmly accepted by others."

President Butler of Columbia University used to tell the students that the only trouble with youth is that it comes so early in life. Youth would be more interesting and enjoyable if it came after there had been sufficient experience of life to increase its enjoyment. And that is what we suggest here —that you can be young in achievement and old in background. What a combination for both youth and age!

{20

Your Golden Age and Your Golden Opportunity

THE OTHER NIGHT I heard time stomping across the world. But it was for just a moment—a moment of confetti, and church bells, and pistol shots, and mad hilarity. Then it was gone, and we were in a new year. Time had marched by. This one mad instant was retreating into the past. For once, I had a sense of movement as if time were really passing before me.

This night the future came to me without any desire on my part. At the stroke of twelve on this New Year's eve, I could hardly make out whether I was marching into the future or the future was coming smack up against me without my knowing it. Somehow I sensed that it was the latter. Some people were out waving rattles, or hurling balls of unwinding paper, or firing revolvers, or ringing church bells.

[271]

They were compromising, as it were, with clock time, or, feeling that it was perhaps useless to resist, were actually trying to help the New Year in. They were making the New Year their event. When certain things happen that we think ourselves powerless to resist, we sometimes jump in and help them along, just to be on the winning side. But I was lying in bed, having no particular wish to compromise on the matter, and sensing that what was happening was the future coming to me without any seeking on my part.

How often it is like that! The future coming without desire. We look at it blinded or dismayed. "That's not our future," we say to ourselves. "*We* didn't order it. It must be someone else's delivered to us by mistake." We'd like to call up Destiny, Incorporated, and say: "Take it back, please."

The future is made up of events, things that someone creates and puts into our existence. But whenever something is created, be it even a simple invention, the results radiate outward indefinitely.

For instance, we invented talking motion pictures. We enjoyed them. It was a fine idea. Immediately the results of that invention spread out wavelike. It was not just the moving picture theaters which, one by one, installed such equipment. Orchestras in individual theaters were dimissed. Organists suffered and found themselves out of positions. Organ builders could not sell organs, and the stockholders and bankers of organ companies were affected. And because there was not as much career opportunity for pupils, music teachers and music schools suffered. Each of these happenings spread outward in its own design. Orchestra players and organists had families; they had to cut down on rent and food, and soon landlords and grocers were affected, even if in small degree.

The effects of the creation of this new idea radiated out in all directions, and new wave centers were to be found on far horizons. Obviously, it would have been a happy situation if each individual affected could have taken a step into the future and created something for himself. Many of them did; many did not.

Today we have the electric organ. Will this new idea of a low-priced manual and pedal organ in the home popularize organ instruction and again fill the pocketbooks of the teachers? Will organ builders envision a modified pipe organ in every home?

But while the theater musicians were suffering, the theaters were prospering because people liked talking pictures. Talking pictures, however, were not immune to competitive ideas. Along came television. Many theaters were abandoned. Other theaters were lucky to fill the first floor, let alone the balconies. Small stores saw their trade dwindle because the passing theater crowds had gone. Owners of some theater buildings found themselves with white elephants. Mortgage holders became worried.

Television has been doing to motion pictures what talking pictures once did to the theater musicians. So the motion picture industry has had to scurry around to find some means of rescuing itself from depression. It has come up with larger screens and three-dimension pictures—really the old idea of the stereoscope that we looked through when children. The great questions are: "Will 3-D or other new processes solve the problem of the moving picture companies? Will the television people then have to offer color,

[273]

larger screens, and more fascinating programs? Or will both prosper?"

Let us take another example. Suppose we put through an express highway between Squeegee City and Dillapsville. The first influence is the creation of a bus line. Then come the trucks. The Poopah Valley railroad that has served the communities so many years begins to suffer. It first takes off two of its four trains, discharges some of its employees, eliminates its dividend and its bond interest, and finally suspends operations. Even Mother Allison, who has had her widow's saving invested in the Poopah bonds, must take in boarders. Trilleytown, which the new highway missed by a few miles, fades away.

Each of the 50 families in Trilleytown must create something else. The schools along the railroad right of way no longer receive tax money from the railroad. They cut the teachers' pay, and the teachers helping to support brothers away at college are no longer able to do so. But, in comes the traveling livestock buyer, a truck gardener takes advantage of the moist land in the bottoms and the new quick transportation, boys establish newspaper routes, the stores in Squeegee City and Dillapsville take on more employees, a dozen filling stations spring up and a host of interesting things transpire incident to the building of just 50 miles of highway. Hundreds of families are ultimately affected in one way or another. If the people are ingenious, creative, and quick to invent a new way of living, well and good; if not, the radiating effects of that new road between Squeegee City and Dillapsville become painful.

But wait a few years. It is not over yet. Here comes the super-super six-lane highway. And now it is no farther in minutes to the Big City twenty miles beyond Dillapsville than it used to be just to Dillapsville. The Dillapsville stores are beginning to feel the pressure of waning trade.

But is it all over now for Dillapsville? No, for now a little later the Big City is getting so crowded that people cannot find parking space. The stores in the Big City are worried that out-of-town customers will no longer buy of them. To add to the problem someone has pictured what atom bombs would do to the Big City.

So here come the residents of the Big City establishing suburban homes near Dillapsville. Dillapsville begins to be talked about as if it were only a suburb of the Big City. Here are motels, restaurants, chain stores, and even branches of department stores growing up in the vicinity of Dillapsville. Dillapsville begins to take on a new look. Even Trilleytown finds its acres cut into suburban home sites.

If all this seems fanciful, take a look at what has been happening around Washington, D.C. I can remember when Silver Springs was just a pleasant little village. Now people even go there to take the railroad train instead of going to the Washington Union Station.

An owner of extensive real estate in Los Angeles tells me that one of the great investment problems there is the rapidity of change. New sections and new shopping centers blossom out in all directions. Older sections speedily are relegated to the background as people seek the new. Whereas in older cities two or three generations might elapse before there was significant change, 20 years is often the limit today. "My corner druggist is already complaining that his business is slipping, and he has been in his locality only 20 years," remarked the investor.

[275]

There are thousands and thousands of such things happening throughout America all the time. Today there are more men in new jobs than ever before, more women working at new things. But there are still newer ideas on the wing. War periods and post-war periods become whirlwinds of new ideas.

The greatest of all industrial ideas of this century is now at hand—atomic power. What a revolution it may turn out to be when ships and railway trains, electric power plants and factories, and even airplanes and automobiles are run by it!

Ideas, as we have said before, travel swiftly these days. The use of atomic power for a submarine took less than ten years from the memorable day when mimeographed papers were handed to the press at the White House pronouncing that we had an atom bomb and that Hiroshima had been destroyed.

Worry over atom bombs falling on factories and cities might in the long run prove minor indeed compared with worry over atomic power changing the nature of entire industries and occupations. When one sees the results of single bombs on Hiroshima and Nagasaki, as I have, one realizes that today we have tremendous power in easily portable form. What might not that do to transportation and the world itself?

But the more startling and revolutionary ideas that are carried into reality, the more ideas each one of us must have. Each idea upsets other well-established ideas, and individuals have to do something about it. We may call it making readjustments, but what it simply means is finding an idea to help ourselves.

Are we to make our own future, or must we permit others to make our future and force us to accept it? How much of your life is *your* life and how much someone else's? How much can you claim as your very own?

Some individuals have stepped into the future, definitely, precisely, and with great consequences to themselves and to others. Such are the men and women most often mentioned in history. They made history because they changed things. And in the changing of things, they changed people as well. Millions, who were perfectly content to play follow the leader, in reality saw their futures unfold only as the leader unfolded them.

Plenty of people make changes for you, but why don't you make some for yourself? Everyone should have a few ideas cooking away for the future. I can't guarantee that they will all work out, but, if one out of five works, you may have completely changed your future.

You will find that nothing gives you such a zest for life and a feeling of accomplishment as to have an idea simmering here and there. Only with ideas can you build security.

Man discovered his future when he found that he could change it. Two or three generations ago, he was all but prohibited from having a future; today he must create one if he is to survive. He must make events. Other people's futures are unsatisfactory. To enjoy and profit from life, the events must be yours.

These techniques of creative thinking I have outlined are the real secret of successful living. Try them, use them regularly, and see for yourself the results they can bring.

You can make *your* world a new world with ideas. Success to you!

Index

Klauder, Charles Zeller, 34
Koch, Robert, 86
Kolodny, Joseph, 241
Kool-Aid, 30
Kroehler Manufacturing Company, 60

Laënnec, René, 154
Lawrence, David, 11
Leahy, Emmet J., 267
Leddy Book and Saddle Shop, 62
Lee, James B., 65
Lee, Robert E., 168
Leedy, Herman U., 158
Leonardo da Vinci, 245-246
Letters of Contrary Opinion, 162, 163
Levand, Max, 231
Levitt, Abraham, 68-69
Library of Congress, 226
 Copyright Office, 226
 Register of Copyrights, 227
Lieurance, Thurlow, 38
Life, 213
Lincoln, Abraham, 168
Lincoln, J. F., 116
Lincoln Electric, 116
Lincoln (Neb.) High School, 133
Lister, Joseph, 86
Logic, 92
London, University of, 12
Long, Dr. Crawford, 232
Los Angeles Chamber of Commerce, 95
Lucchese, Cosimo, 63
Luce, Henry, 198
 Life, 213
 Time, 198-199, 200
Lurton, Douglas, 116

MacAndrews & Forbes, 120-121
McEvoy, J. P., 179
Magazines (*see* Periodicals)
Maglio, Dominick, 184-185
Magnificent Obsession, The, 208
Maharajah of Jaipur, 39
Mail order, 199

Manet, Edouard, 194
Marconi, Guglielmo, 42
Marcus, Stanley, 37
Marden, Orison Swett, 166, 173
 Pushing to the Front, 166, 173
Markham, Edwin, 264
Massachusetts Institute of Technology, 20, 115
May, Robert L., 242
 Rudolph the Red-Nosed Reindeer, 242
Memory, 158
Mendel, Abbot J. G., 244
Mental efficiency, 175
Mental fatigue, 176-177
Merchandising, 170
Merck & Company, 120
Metropolitan Museum of Art (*see* Museums)
Miami, University of, 121
Middle Age, 32
Military secrets, 14
Miller, Dr. Benjamin, 155
Milton, John, 264
Milwaukee Railroad, 63
Minnesota Mining and Manufacturing Company, 62
Mohammed Ali, 25
Montgomery Ward, 242
Moore, Robert L., 248
Morse, Samuel, 42, 73
Munsey, Frank A., 166
Murdock, Victor, 147
Museums:
 Brooklyn Museum, 38
 Costume Institute, 38
 Crocker Art Gallery, 152
 Metropolitan Museum of Art, 38
 Museum of New Mexico Art Gallery, 36
Mutual Security Administration, 211

National Association of Suggestion Systems, 15
National Inventors Council, 13, 100, 159, 189
National Research Development Corporation (*see* Great Britain)

[283]

THE AUTHOR AND HIS BOOK

ROBERT PLATT CRAWFORD, Professor of Journalism at the University of Nebraska, was born in Council Bluffs, Iowa, in 1893. Educated at Nebraska, where he received his A.B., and Columbia University, where he took an A.M., he was a reporter on the *Nebraska State Journal,* an assistant editor in the United States Department of Agriculture at Washington, and associate editor of the *Nebraska Farmer* before joining the University of Nebraska faculty. He has been Professor of Journalism at Nebraska since 1926 and established his pioneering course in creative thinking there in 1931. In 1940–41, Professor Crawford was visiting professor of journalism at the University of Texas. From 1944 to 1948, he served as a specialist on business and finance with the Office of War Information; as a member of the faculty of the Army University, Florence, Italy; and in various capacities with General Douglas Mac-Arthur's occupation staff in Japan. He has traveled extensively in Europe, Siberia, Manchuria and Japan. His previous books include *These Fifty Years* (University of Nebraska, 1925), *The Magazine Article* (McGraw-Hill, 1931) and *Think for Yourself* (McGraw-Hill, 1937 – now a Fraser Publishing Company reprint).